Conquering
Post-Traumatic
Stress Disorder

"Drs. Beckner and Arden have pulled together the most effective, evidence-based methods for treating trauma that science knows of to date."

—Josef Ruzek, Ph.D., U.S. Department of Veteran's Affairs
National Center for Posttraumatic Stress Disorder

Conquering
Post-Traumatic
Stress Disorder

The Newest Techniques for
Overcoming Symptoms, Regaining Hope,
and Getting Your Life Back

VICTORIA LEMLE BECKNER, PH.D.,
AND JOHN B. ARDEN, PH.D.

FAIR WINDS
PRESS
BEVERLY, MASSACHUSETTS

Text © 2008 Victoria Lemle Beckner, Ph.D. and John B. Arden, Ph.D.

First published in the USA in 2008 by
Fair Winds Press, a member of
Quayside Publishing Group
100 Cummings Center
Suite 406-L
Beverly, MA 01915-6101
www.fairwindspress.com

The information in this book is for educational purposes only. It is not intended to replace the advice of a physician or medical practitioner. Please see your health care provider before beginning any new health program.

12 11 10 09 08   1 2 3 4 5

ISBN-13: 978-1-59233-309-7
ISBN-10: 1-59233-309-5

Library of Congress Cataloging-in-Publication Data

Beckner, Victoria.
    Conquering post-traumatic stress disorder : the newest techniques for overcoming symptoms, regaining hope, and getting your life back / Victoria Lemle Beckner and John B. Arden.
        p. cm.
    Includes index.
    ISBN-13: 978-1-59233-309-7
    1. Post-traumatic stress disorder–Popular works.   I. Arden, John B. II. Title.
    RC552.P67L43 2008
    616.85′21–dc22

                                                            2008018300

Cover design by Howard Grossman/12E Design
Book design by Dutton and Sherman Designs

Printed and bound in USA

For my husband, Russell, and in memory of my dad, Morton Beckner

—Victoria

This book is dedicated to my late father.

—John

Contents

INTRODUCTION

Trauma is a life-changing experience. Whether the event is a car accident, earthquake, combat, sexual abuse, fire, or shooting—in that moment you are transformed. While many people recover over time from a traumatic experience, others continue to struggle with painful memories, nightmares, feeling "on guard," avoiding certain situations, physical difficulties, depression, and emotional numbing. These are the common symptoms of Post-Traumatic Stress Disorder (PTSD).

If you have experienced a trauma, you might recognize some of these problems in yourself. You may also have trouble working, going to school, or taking care of your duties at home. And just when you really need support, you find that your relationships are strained and distant as well. Finally, trauma challenges your fundamental system of beliefs about who you are, your ability to trust and relate to others, and how you view the world.

So how do you work through this, and find your way back to your life?

The good news is that in the last two decades, mental health clinicians and researchers have been working together to develop effective techniques for overcoming PTSD. While there are many approaches out there to treating trauma, not all have been shown in research studies to reduce PTSD symptoms and improve mood and quality of life. How do you know what really works? Whether you are seeking a psychotherapist or shopping for a self-help book, you want to find out if there are data backing the approach.

In *Conquering Post-Traumatic Stress Disorder*, we have selected the most up-to-date, evidence-based strategies for treating PTSD. Included throughout are the key skills, tools, and knowledge that have been shown to be highly effective interventions—and therefore provide the greatest return for your efforts. These include cognitive-behavioral techniques designed to help you reduce anxiety and anger, increase your pleasure and social activities, and overcome your avoidance of places and situations that have shrunk your world. And because people with PTSD often withdraw from family and friends, we have included evidence-based relationship strategies to teach you how to develop better communication and conflict-resolution skills to reestablish connection with others. Through step-by-step exercises, we teach you how to be your own therapist.

We have also included powerful techniques for working through your traumatic memory. Many self-help books (and therapists) shy away from this work because facing the trauma memory is a frightening and painful process. This is also the reason people with PTSD often avoid any reminders of their trauma. But research suggests that to overcome PTSD, you must emotionally process the experience using some form of "exposure" therapy that involves thinking, talking, or writing about the trauma memory. While it is ideal to work with a therapist on trauma-focused work, we can show you how to do it on your own. This book provides you the tools for working through the trauma memory in a manner that is structured, controlled, and safe.

Finally, overcoming PTSD is not merely a fight to abolish the negative symptoms of trauma—there is also tremendous potential for growth. Many people who have survived a trauma discover in themselves new strengths, achieve a heightened appreciation for life and their relationships, and develop new life goals. Unfortunately, the field often neglects this potential for post-traumatic growth. But each person has his or her own unique form of resiliency, and it is essential for you to recognize and nurture yours. For this reason we have devoted the final chapter to the topic of growing from trauma, although the theme of self-transformation runs throughout the book.

Conquering your PTSD requires daily courage and effort. Many of the skills and exercises in this book will be challenging, but the path from trauma to recovery and growth can be a deeply meaningful and empowering journey.

SECTION 1

What Is Post-Traumatic Stress Disorder?

CHAPTER 1

Six Trauma Survivors: Their Stories

In this chapter, you'll meet six people who have experienced trauma and have developed Post-Traumatic Stress Disorder (PTSD) as a result. While these particular individuals are fictitious, their cases are based on clients we have worked with over the years; identifying details have been changed to protect their anonymity. "Sonya," "Dan," "Nicole," "Barry," "Angela," and "Ian" will be your companions on your journey through this book, as you travel from trauma to recovery.

Sonya: Auto Accident

Sonya, a loan officer at a bank in a town outside of Chicago, was driving to her office one morning when it began to snow. As she exited the freeway, she could feel her car begin to slide. Suddenly, the car skidded off the ramp and rolled over, tumbling down the embankment. To Sonya, it felt as though the accident was happening in slow motion. When her car stopped, it was upside down and she was trapped, her left arm crushed. The hot chocolate she had been drinking dripped from the ceiling as she waited in terror for help.

Sonya was hospitalized with several broken ribs, and her left arm sustained multiple fractures and nerve damage. Sonya's ex-husband took care of their eight-year-old son, Eric, while she was in the hospital.

When she was discharged, she knew something was wrong beyond her serious physical injuries. She was having nightmares about the accident, and felt anxious all the time. Her friend Laura and several coworkers checked in with her periodically during the several months she was on disability leave, but Sonya didn't want to see anybody. She had family in New Mexico, but she discouraged them from coming out to help. She felt strange and disoriented, as if the world had suddenly been stripped bare, revealing itself as a precarious and dangerous place.

Because of her injury, Sonya had to learn how to do her household chores and other activities with one hand. She relearned how to get dressed, cook, and type with just her right hand. But Sonya was terrified of learning how to drive again, which meant that she had to depend on her ex-husband to take Eric to school and soccer practice. She felt ashamed of her fear, and often helpless as a mother.

Dan: Combat in Iraq

Dan was a thirty-five-year-old Army soldier who served two tours in Iraq, the last time in Baghdad. He saw a lot of combat, especially when his unit tried to secure a new area. Security patrols were also dangerous because of snipers and the improvised explosive devices (IEDs) on the roads.

During one of these patrols, the Humvee in front of Dan's hit an undetected IED. It was carrying his close buddy Cesar and three other soldiers he knew well. The explosion was followed by sniper fire, and Dan ran forward to help while his fellow soldiers returned fire. When Dan got to the smoking Humvee, he found that Cesar had been mortally wounded; the other three sustained injuries, but survived.

When Dan returned to his hometown near Fort Hood, Texas, after his second tour was over, he was edgy, numb, and irritable with his wife, Heather. He was relieved to be back, but life felt strange on the home front. He couldn't relate to the day-to-day things that seemed important to others, and he missed the feeling of intensity and the sense of purpose he'd had while on active duty. He was also plagued by gruesome images of Cesar's body, and guilt that he survived while others died.

The months dragged by. Dan couldn't let down his guard anywhere. Groups of people made him intensely anxious, and he started avoiding crowded coffee shops, bars, and shopping centers. He began smoking pot during the day to "chill out." Most nights, he drank to get to sleep and woke up exhausted. Fights with Heather had become so frequent and intense that she threatened to move out.

Nicole: Childhood Abuse

Nicole was an only child who lived with her parents in Omaha, Nebraska. Her father's brother and his wife lived nearby, and visited frequently. When Nicole was seven years old, her uncle started to spend more time alone with her, giving her a lot of desired attention and physical affection. She adored him, and felt safe and comfortable in his presence.

Slowly, her uncle's touching started to make Nicole feel strange and afraid. She tried to avoid him, but he continued to find ways of sexually abusing her for years. He told her to keep their secret "relationship" to herself, and that her parents wouldn't like what she was doing. His words deepened her shame, and she didn't tell anyone about what was happening.

Nicole withdrew inside herself, often feeling detached from her life and from others. Sometimes when she was with her uncle, she would feel as if she were outside her body and lose track of time. Later, she learned that this feeling was called dissociation, a way of mentally escaping the situation. Her parents commented on her quiet and sometimes sour disposition. They signed her up for piano lessons, dance classes, and school plays, trying to get her more engaged with life and other kids. Reluctantly, Nicole went along with their efforts.

By the time she was in middle school, Nicole had learned to avoid her uncle by leaving home whenever he and his wife visited. She grew into a guarded teenager with few close friends. Though she struggled internally with anxiety, shame, rage, and low self-esteem, she put on a tough exterior. She kept people physically and emotionally distant with her edgy sarcasm and serious demeanor. Because Nicole worked hard in school and did well, her parents assumed she was okay.

In college, she was able to get closer than usual to several women friends, but her occasional angry flare-ups would sometimes drive people away. She struggled with dating and had a panic attack the first time she became sexual with a boyfriend she'd been seeing for a month. After college, she continued to date without much success—she felt mistrustful of her partners, and the physical part of the relationships always triggered anxiety and avoidance in her.

It was not until Nicole was thirty-seven years old that she finally met someone—Peter—with whom she felt she could let down her guard. Hopeful that she might finally be getting past her history, Nicole became engaged to Peter after they'd been together two years. But as they grew closer, Nicole discovered that her memories of abuse were surfacing stronger than ever, and with them, intense anger and anxiety.

Barry: Fatal Fire

Barry had been a firefighter for twenty-one years when one day he and his company were called to respond to a series of fires that were spreading out of control in Southern California. He was working in a neighborhood that was in danger of burning, helping to evacuate residents. Suddenly the hot, dry Santa Ana winds turned eastward, rapidly driving the flames toward the neighborhood. As people were scrambling to flee, they told Barry about a woman who was trapped upstairs in her home. Barry ran toward the house, and when he entered, he was almost overcome by the smoke and heat. He could hear the woman screaming from the second floor, but the stairs had given way and he could only call to her, asking if she was alone in the house. She was.

Barry and his team tried desperately to rescue the woman. On the roof, they broke through a window in the one spot where fire wasn't consuming the second floor, but inside the room was ablaze. They could not get inside the house, and she could not get out. Slowly Barry realized that an impenetrable wall of fire and smoke hopelessly separated him from the woman. They had tried everything, but he couldn't save her. Barry and his team had to move on and continue clearing other residents out of the area.

Barry was haunted by this fire and by the death of the woman he had never met. While others had died in the regional fires, the woman's death felt personal to him. She had screamed for his help, and he couldn't save her. He felt he had failed in his duty.

Barry's captain told him to take some time off, but it didn't help. Images of flames and crumbling stairs kept intruding into his thoughts, and a feeling of helplessness and doom darkened his mood. Sometimes, he would break into tears, then quickly pull himself together. Other times he just felt emotionally flat, and lacked motivation to do anything. Already a quiet man, Barry withdrew from his wife, Shaundra, and their two daughters. He stopped socializing with his colleagues at the fire station. Whenever he was called out to an emergency, he felt shaky and uncertain. He had lost faith in his power to protect others.

Angela: Hurricane Katrina

Angela was living with her brother and his family in New Orleans when Hurricane Katrina hit. They had stayed in the city hoping to ride out the storm, as they had many times before. But this time, the levees broke and flooded their neighborhood. They narrowly escaped to the roof of their home. After waiting helplessly for a day, they were rescued by boat and taken to the Superdome.

Meanwhile, their mother was trapped in a retirement home in a different part of the city, and Angela could not get any information about the facility. After her brother's family was transported to Baton Rouge and Angela went to Houston to stay with her sister, the family learned that no one had been evacuated from the retirement facility. Eventually, Angela's mother's body was recovered from the wreckage.

Angela's anxiety did not go away once she was safe in Houston, and it was compounded by intense grief over her mother's death and the sweeping loss of her lifelong community and home. Rainy days kept her in bed all day, fighting the memories of her world disappearing under water, and imagining her mother's death. She was also disturbed by an underlying sense of dread and waves of anxiety symptoms, including dizziness and trouble breathing. Sometimes she would have spontaneous panic attacks and thought she would faint or die of a heart attack. This made it difficult for her to keep her temporary jobs, and she started avoiding buses and other situations where she feared she might be trapped.

Eventually, Angela gave up working and stayed close to home, taking care of her sister's toddler. Before the trauma, Angela was known for her high spirits and busy productivity, whether at home or at the restaurant where she worked. But Katrina had stripped away her enthusiasm for life and her sense of purpose, and shaken her religious faith. Two years after the hurricane, she still couldn't regain a sense of safety or normalcy.

Ian: Assault and Robbery

Ian was four years out of college and working his first job as a software programmer for a firm in New York City. One evening after a particularly long and exhausting day of work, he walked toward his car in the underground garage of his office building. When he clicked his remote key to unlock the car door, the headlights blinked, revealing two men sitting in his car. Ian froze.

After what seemed like an eternity, Ian's legs started working and he turned to run. The men got out of the car and chased him through the garage. When they grabbed him, Ian saw that they were teenagers. They took his wallet, keys, and watch before they beat him up and sped off in his car. A few minutes later, a coworker found Ian conscious but badly injured on the floor of the garage and called 911.

Ian recovered physically from the assault, but not emotionally. He was anxious in his apartment and installed a costly alarm system he couldn't afford. It took him hours to fall asleep. After finally getting to sleep, he would wake four or five hours later, exhausted and irritable, often covered with sweat from a nightmare.

Sometimes Ian would stay with his parents on Long Island just to get some rest. He felt deeply ashamed for freezing during the assault and not being able to defend himself. He returned to work a week after the assault, but he couldn't concentrate or remember what happened in meetings. Finally, his boss talked to him about getting treatment for PTSD.

■

Although these six people experienced very different kinds of trauma, they ended up with very similar problems. They all struggled with intrusive memories of the event, such as nightmares, flashbacks, and unwanted thoughts and images. Their nervous systems seemed to be stuck on ready alert much of the time: they were jumpy, edgy, hyper-vigilant for danger, and had trouble concentrating and sleeping. All tended to avoid situations or cues that reminded them of the trauma, and most felt numb or estranged from the people in their lives. These are the common symptoms of Post-Traumatic Stress Disorder (PTSD).

What Is a Trauma?

Everyone has experienced stressful events, such as having to give an important presentation at work, getting into a fight with one's spouse, being in a minor accident, getting caught in storm, or even going to the doctor. These experiences are stressful because they threaten to some degree one's physical, social, or emotional well-being.

A trauma involves facing an unusually severe threat. It is a highly stressful event in which one's life, health, or emotional security is seriously threatened or harmed, although it can also involve witnessing the death of or serious threat to another. Traumas have a much deeper impact on one's well-being than a typical stressor, and can take a long time to recover from.

Traumas can come about in several ways. **Natural traumas** are caused by natural disasters such as Hurricanes Katrina and Rita, tornados that rip through towns in the Midwest, fires that threaten your home or neighborhood, major earthquakes, or floods. Other natural traumas include experiencing a life-threatening illness, such as stroke or heart attack, or seeing a loved one go through the end stages of cancer or Alzheimer's disease.

Traumas can also be brought about by events that are caused by humans, either accidentally or intentionally. **Unintentional traumas** include accidents such as an explosion in a plant, the collapse of a bridge or building, or a serious car accident. Particularly vulnerable to the effects of unintentional traumas are first-responders. Firefighters, police, emergency medical teams, and disaster-response workers regularly confront life-threatening situations, cope with threats to their own lives, and witness death and serious injuries.

Intentional traumas are generally the most psychologically damaging. Intentional traumas are human acts of violence such as physical abuse, shootings, assault, kidnapping, terrorism, war, or torture. Many of our combat troops are returning from Iraq and Afghanistan with PTSD after experiencing multiple life-threatening attacks as well as having to kill others.

People can also respond with intense fear or horror to an event that, objectively, may not seem as threatening as those listed above. For example, discovering that a spouse is having an affair would make anyone furious and upset. But for some, such an event may threaten one's entire sense of trust and meaning, taking on a traumatic quality.

Part of what makes any experience traumatic is how you interpret both the event itself and your ability to cope with it. Different people can be present at the same event at the same time, yet each person's experience and response will be unique. Any intense trauma can lead to PTSD, but it's important to recognize that every trauma survivor brings his or her own meaning—and way of coping—to the event, based on personal history, personality, strengths, weaknesses, skills, and relationships. And while it is clear that the enormity of a trauma has caused something to go wrong in the mind, brain, and body of someone with PTSD, every individual struggling with this disorder also has his or her own unique source of resiliency to draw upon for recovery.

Moving Forward

Perhaps you have experienced a traumatic event and recognize in yourself some of the symptoms of PTSD. If so, the fact that you've picked up this book probably means you are tired of being trapped by your fear and ruled by your symptoms. You are ready to take on recovery. But as you probably know by now, the road back to emotional health and well-being is a difficult one after a trauma. It takes tremendous courage as well as hard work, including doing some things you may not want to do.

This book, and the experiences of the six individuals introduced in this chapter, can help you on your brave journey. We invite you to tap into your strengths, master the skills needed to fight PTSD, and reclaim the joy and vitality of your life. Congratulations on taking your first steps.

Find a Good Notebook for Journaling

You should get yourself a notebook or journal dedicated to your PTSD work. You will need the journal for doing a number of the exercises in this book, and to keep track of your thoughts and any ideas you want to remember as you read. Having everything together in one notebook will also provide you a record of your progress.

CHAPTER 2

What Is Post-Traumatic Stress?

People with PTSD usually don't understand what is happening to their minds or bodies. Sonya thought she was losing her mind. Ian thought his symptoms were a sign of his emotional and moral weakness. Feelings of shame, despair, and confusion are common. Often, people attempt to cope with their symptoms in counterproductive ways that perpetuate the problem, such as soothing themselves with alcohol or drugs, avoiding the situations that make them anxious, or withdrawing from relationships.

When you're suffering from PTSD, the short answer to what's going on inside your head and body is that your healthy stress system has been strained by trauma; in this context, all the resulting symptoms make perfect sense. The good news is that we actually know a lot about how post-traumatic stress develops and what causes its symptoms. This knowledge is important to your recovery.

In this chapter, you'll learn about the normal reactions to stress and trauma, including the physical, psychological, and behavioral reactions that are part of our adaptive "fight-or-flight" stress alarm systems. Everyone has this stress alarm system—we've all experienced the physical and emotional alarm responses that are triggered when we're faced with a furious spouse, sit for a final exam, or see a child wandering into traffic. The symptoms of PTSD develop when your alarm system response goes into overdrive and overwhelms your brain in a life-threatening or horrific situation. Such situations disrupt the formation of your memory of the events and keep your alarm system on active alert, even after the danger has passed.

Understanding how a normal stress system works will help you understand what happens when you add trauma to the mix, and how the PTSD symptoms arise and what they mean. Because having that knowledge can help take the mystery, fear, and unpredictability out of your symptoms, consider this chapter your first intervention for overcoming PTSD!

Your Body's Stress Alarm System

Anything that you interpret as a threat or danger will trigger your body's stress alarm system. Suppose a car crosses head-on into your lane of traffic, or that you slip while you're walking along a cliff-hugging trail high above a canyon. It's a very good thing that your brain instantly recognizes these situations as potentially dangerous, so that you swerve out of the oncoming car's path, or grab a branch so you don't tumble down the cliff.

You are literally "wired" to quickly sense any physical or emotional threat to you or the people you care about, and your brain is designed to respond by setting off your alarm system to cope with that threat. Once triggered, your alarm system causes the release of stress hormones to pump you into action, directs your mind to identify and focus on the threat, and elicits anxiety or fear which motivates coping, escape, or fight behavior. It's easy to see how all this happens when you are faced with an immediate physical threat such as a crash or falling off a cliff. But your alarm system is also triggered when you anticipate a threat in the future, such as having to give an important presentation at work or take a final exam.

Anxiety and fear, which are associated with your body's alarm response, are adaptive and necessary. These emotions drive you to do certain behaviors that help you deal with the threat, such as freezing, running, rescuing someone, arguing, fighting, or working harder.

The level of threat determines the intensity of the alarm response and the associated emotion:

- Threats in the future, such as an upcoming final exam, will activate your alarm system and cause moderate anxiety, motivating you to study harder.

- Immediate threats, such as a potentially violent confrontation, will trigger a high alarm response, intense anxiety, and behaviors geared toward defending your position.

- An immediate life-threatening event, such as a near-miss car accident, will create a red-alert alarm response: fear and/or anxiety intense enough to trigger a panic attack, and an immediate fight-or-flight action such as swerving away from the oncoming car.

How Your Alarm System Works

We know a lot about what happens in the brain and body when your alarm system is activated. In his 1929 book, *Bodily Changes in Pain, Hunger, Fear and Rage,* Harvard professor Walter Cannon first drew attention to the fight-or-flight stress response. This response involves *real* physiological changes; anyone who tells you that you're imagining your symptoms of anxiety, stress, and trauma is absolutely wrong.

Let's take a closer look at exactly what happens to your brain and body when you are faced with a challenge or a threat.

Gearing Up for Action

Whether you are facing a growling pit bull or a contentious boss, the moment your brain detects the threat, it hits the stress alarm system button. This sets off a chain of physiological events in your body to ready you for action. These changes include increasing the amount of oxygen you breathe, redirecting blood flow to your muscles, quickly boosting blood sugar levels to provide you with energy, and initiating a behavioral urgency to act. The stress alarm system actually activates two systems: a "fast" system to deal with the threat immediately, and a "slow" system to maintain readiness over the longer term.

The fast sympathetic nervous system is the first to kick into action in response to a threat. This system engages as soon as you see the angry dog or surly boss; your brain directly stimulates internal organs via sympathetic nerves and also releases the hormone adrenalin in order to initiate the fight-or-flight response. The sympathetic-adrenalin response has a widespread effect on your body, intended to prepare you for immediate action. Physiological changes include increases in heart rate, blood pressure, and oxygen flow through respiratory pathways. Blood is moved away from your skin, liver, and digestive system and toward your heart, muscles, and lungs to deliver more oxygen and glucose to these areas. Adrenalin also makes you feel more alert and ready—it's what we call hypervigilance—a sense of being on edge, keeping an eye out for danger, or startling easily.

The second system to be activated during the stress response is the Hypothalamus-Pituitary-Adrenal (HPA) cortex system. Unlike the fast adrenalin response, the HPA stress response relies on the relatively slower action of steroid hormones such as cortisol to exert their effects. Cortisol plays a critical role in raising circulating levels of sugar in your blood to provide energy to your muscles and brain for the ongoing stress response. If you ever wondered how you could keep going for hours during a very stressful or traumatic event, you can thank cortisol. It's also what keeps firefighters awake and effective for days, students from passing out during a test after studying all night, and (unfortunately) arguing spouses from calming down and talking through a conflict.

Physical Symptoms

Both the fast sympathetic-adrenalin response and the slower cortisol response cause changes in your body that enable you to cope with a threat or danger. They may feel like scary symptoms to you, but they are important physical responses that everyone experiences when confronting a threat that triggers stress or anxiety:

- *Racing heart:* Your heart rate and blood pressure increase in order to get more blood and oxygen to the muscles. Blood is redirected away from your hands and feet, which is why these extremities can feel cold and look pale.

- *Hyperventilation:* Your breathing increases (hyperventilation) to get more oxygen into the blood. This can cause sensations of breathlessness, choking, or chest pain brought on by tension in the chest muscles.

- *Sweating:* Perspiration cools your overheated body.

- *Light-headed, dizziness, weakness:* When your breathing accelerates, it causes a decrease in carbon dioxide in the blood which changes the blood's pH balance, making it more alkaline. This change is not dangerous, but it can cause unpleasant physical symptoms such as light-headedness, dizziness, hot flashes, or feeling weak as if you haven't eaten.

- *Sense of unreality:* Changes in oxygen flow and blood pH can cause you to have feelings of unreality or confusion. You feel strange, detached, ungrounded.

- *Hunger and digestion:* Your digestive system shuts down, often decreasing your appetite or causing stomach pain or diarrhea. You may stop eating, or may over-eat to calm yourself.

- *Muscle tension and pain:* Muscles all over your body tighten up to prepare for flight or fight, resulting in a feeling of tension and pain.

- *Shivering:* To maximize blood flow to vital organs, your blood drains away from your skin. As blood vessels constrict, you may find yourself shivering, because without blood flow to your skin, the surface area becomes colder and you get goose bumps.

- *Blurred vision:* Your pupils widen to let in more light, which can also cause blurred vision or sensitivity to light.

- *Mental vigilance:* Your attention narrows to focus on potential threats, and you become hypervigilant, scanning the environment for danger.

- *Shaking and jitteriness:* The flow of adrenalin and your focus on danger can make you shake or feel jumpy and easily startled. It can also make you irritable.

- *Urge to act:* When the danger alert system is activated, your brain generates an overwhelming urge to act, either to escape or to aggressively defend yourself. It is very difficult simply to stay in the situation or continue what you are doing.

Panic Attacks—An Extreme Response

A panic attack occurs when the threat feels immediate and especially severe, triggering your alarm system into maximum gear. The physical and emotional symptoms of the alarm system will be very intense, and often cause even more anxiety and panic. It is important to realize, however, that while a panic attack feels pretty overwhelming and scary, it is simply an extreme alarm system response: Your body is designed to handle it. If you attribute the symptoms to a greater problem—for example, thinking that you're having a heart attack—you'll react with even greater fear, exacerbating the symptoms.

These Responses Are Normal

While everyone has these alarm system responses, including occasional panic attacks, many people find them frightening. Anxiety is, after all, a very uncomfortable feeling. Your brain is shouting *Danger!*—even if there is none—and the physical sensations can make you feel like you are about to have a heart attack, faint, or lose your mind.

But your body's alarm system is an adaptive system built for responding to a threat, *and the alarm system response itself is not dangerous*. The fact that during a very stressful or traumatic event you may have experienced many of these symptoms does not mean something is wrong (or that you will necessarily develop PTSD). It's important to understand that all of these physical changes serve an important function, and everyone experiences them to a certain degree when faced with a threat.

Turning Off the Alarm System

Under normal circumstances, the stressor or emergency eventually ends. Your body has several systems designed to calm your alarm system and return the brain and body to its non-stressed state. When the snarling dog starts to lick your arm or the boss smiles and says "Good job!" your brain decides that the threat is over, slowing the release of stress hormones. It also causes your parasympathetic nervous system—the system designed to calm your body when the danger is over—to quickly shut down the sympathetic-adrenalin response, slowing your heart rate and relaxing your muscles.

What happens following a trauma, though, is that the brain continues to be prepared for threat, keeping your alarm system on ready alert and never fully turning off. This state of chronic stress has physical consequences. Because your body expends energy when your alarm system is activated, it has to conserve energy in other places, where it can. Various "maintenance" projects in the body—including digestion, tissue repair and growth, energy storage, and reproductive activities—are put on hold until after the emergency. Your immune system also competes for your body's depleted resources, temporarily slowing down during a stressful event, which is why you catch a cold or get sick when you've been stressed for a period of time.

Trauma: Your Stress Alarm System on Overdrive

A trauma isn't normal stress. It involves facing an overwhelming threat or danger, such as being assaulted, watching your house go up in flames, or seeing a loved one have a heart attack. When you experience a traumatic event, your alarm system gets cranked so high that stress hormones such as adrenaline and cortisol literally flood your brain. This interferes with how your brain normally processes an experience to store it as an organized memory. The trauma memory is fragmented into images, smells, and sounds, and is highly emotional. It is like a live wire in your brain, hot and unpredictable. And anything associated with the trauma memory— a face, the sound of a helicopter, a dark corridor, the smell of something burning—can set off your alarm system, reactivating it repeatedly and keeping it on constant alert.

Symptoms of Post-Traumatic Stress Disorder

Now you can understand how the symptoms of PTSD develop. The overwhelming experience of a trauma disrupts the formation of organized memory, leading the trauma victim to re-experience symptoms of PTSD, such as intrusive memories, images, and nightmares. The fragmented memory of the trauma also works to keep your alarm system on ready alert: Any reminders of the trauma will instantly activate the physiological symptoms and emotional responses like anxiety, irritability, or anger. The constant anxiety and intrusive memories often lead to avoidance and numbing symptoms. The American Psychiatric Association's *Diagnostic and Statistical Manual of Mental Disorders, Fourth Edition,* groups these symptoms into three clusters: re-experiencing symptoms, physiological hyperarousal symptoms, and avoidance or numbing. Let's look at the symptoms in more detail.

"Re-Experiencing" Symptoms

When you experience a traumatic event, you often find yourself reliving the experience through unwanted memories of the event. For example, you may have thoughts or images of the trauma that intrude into your mind and feel distressing or uncontrollable. Recurrent nightmares of the event are also common, though in children the content of the dream may be different from the trauma (e.g., monsters). Sometimes a survivor of trauma will suddenly have a sense that he or she is back in the middle of the experience, see-ing and acting out aspects of the event as if it is happening (this is called a "flashback"). Reminders of the trauma will typically trigger anxiety as well, as if you are back in the threatening situation again. These are all called "re-experiencing" symptoms of PTSD.

Why do these re-experiencing symptoms occur? When you have a routine experience such as going to a ball game, your brain pro-cesses that experience and stores it as organized verbal, sensory, and emotional memory networks that are connected in a logical way. Stress hormones enhance memory, so that you will better remember potentially threatening events. But when a trauma causes too much of these chemicals to be released, the parts of the brain that organize and manage memories are overwhelmed and disrupted. The trauma memory becomes a collection of fragmented images and associations, all highly emotional, intruding into your consciousness uncontrollably.

Remember Angela, who survived Hurricane Katrina? She often found that while she was watching television or eating dinner, dis-turbing images of houses under water or of her mother's face would pop into her mind. Trauma memories often involve intense sensory experiences such as sounds, tastes, and smells. Sometimes the experience is so real you feel like you are truly re-experiencing the trauma. Whenever Dan, the soldier who served in Iraq, drove on the highway, the sight of rumbling trucks would take him right back to his convoy in Iraq just before the explosion. Trauma nightmares can also feel startlingly real, causing you to wake up in a cold sweat, unable to shake off the feeling that you are back in the experience.

It is natural for people to attempt to avoid or suppress a trauma memory. But because the memory remains emotionally hot and unprocessed, your brain wants to work it through and organize the experience. The more you try to suppress such memories, the more they keep popping up, intruding into your daily activities and your sleep.

Re-experiencing symptoms are a sign that your body and mind are actively struggling to cope with the traumatic experience and make sense of what has happened. What is needed is a process to reorganize your memory and integrate the associated parts of your brain that are activated whenever you think of the event. Many of the exercises in this book, including talking or writing about the event and overcoming avoidance behaviors, can help you reduce these disturbing symptoms of trauma.

Hyper-Arousal Symptoms

You already know that whenever the stress alarm system is activated, it causes the physiological changes in the body. Because people with PTSD are walking around with their alarm system on constant alert and easily triggered by trauma reminders, they usually experience a variety of physiological symptoms, described above on pages 29–31.

The activation of the stress alarm system also causes a number of additional physiological problems, called "hyper-arousal" symptoms. These include hypervigilance (feeling on edge and alert for danger), feeling jumpy and easily startled, difficulty concentrating, irritability, and insomnia.

While it makes sense that hypervigilance and exaggerated startle are part of the stress response, you may be surprised to learn that hyper-arousal can lead to difficulties with concentration and memory. This occurs because stress causes you to narrow your attention on the threat, making it hard to pay attention to (and therefore remember) the other things going on (conversations, etc.). People also don't realize that irritability and anger are strongly enhanced by an active alarm system. A friend makes a comment and you suddenly snap at him, or you hear a story on the news and find that you're suddenly furious or in tears. Nicole, a survivor of childhood sexual abuse, found that she was easily and unexpectedly agitated and often argued with family members or friends.

The stress hormones involved in the alarm response also disrupt normal sleep patterns, one of the most debilitating problems of PTSD. People who have experienced a trauma often find that they have trouble falling asleep, staying asleep, or feeling rested in the morning. This pattern is made even worse by nightmares, which often keep people up for hours, force them to get up very early in the morning, or even to postpone going to sleep. Such disruptions make you feel tired and irritable during the day, and can seriously interfere with work, school, and family life. You'll learn more about sleep problems in chapter 6.

Whenever someone with PTSD confronts a reminder of the trauma, his or her alarm system kicks into higher gear, causing more noticeable physical symptoms. For Barry, the firefighter, the smell of smoke would suddenly bring on a rapid heartbeat, sweating, shaking, dizziness, tension, and anxiety. Sometimes his reaction was intense enough to trigger a panic attack.

Numbing and Avoidance

While intrusive memories and physical symptoms may be more noticeable in people with PTSD, there is another important set of symptoms that are less obvious but cause just as much impairment. Individuals who have experienced a trauma often shut down emotionally in order to avoid trauma memories and feelings, leading to emotional numbing and avoidance of trauma-related reminders.

If you've gone through a trauma, you know how it feels to be emotionally numb. You feel flat, detached from your life, and no longer interested in the things that used to bring you pleasure such as cooking, sex, playing sports, working in your garden, being with friends, listening to music, or even reading. You may also feel estranged from others, or have difficulty expressing loving feelings.

Numbing occurs because there is no easy way to block out the bad feelings without blocking out *all* feelings, including positive ones such as joy, humor, and love. Numbing also occurs as a result of depression, which commonly develops in people with PTSD. Because of this emotional flatness, people often withdraw from relationships, feeling that they are no longer fulfilling, or fearing that their mood or behavior will put off others. Unfortunately, the more you avoid others and the activities you once enjoyed, the harder life gets. It's another negative spiral—but the good news is, with help you'll get from techniques we talk about in chapter 5, it's something you can change.

It is also common for people to find themselves avoiding certain places, thoughts, conversations, or activities associated with the trauma. Your brain automatically and without any conscious awareness "learns" that anything associated with the trauma is dangerous—it's called conditioning. This might be the location, the date or time of day or even the temperature, colors, sights, sounds, certain people—anything that reminds you of the event. These associations or reminders can trigger the body's alarm system, causing anxiety and physical symptoms. For Sonya, who was in the car accident, driving triggered a conditioned fear response in her. Ian's anxiety level would go up every time he went into a parking garage. Even though the danger has passed, the brain is slow to unlearn these associations and continues to trigger anxiety with any trauma reminder. And whatever triggers anxiety, people naturally start to avoid. Sonya immediately stopped driving after the accident, and only rode the bus because she had to. If it persists, avoidance can have a big impact on your life. You may have a difficult time visiting friends, going to church, traveling far from home, or doing some of the pleasurable activities you once loved to do.

Depression

People who have experienced a traumatic event often develop depression. If you think about it, this makes sense. During the day, you feel anxious but you don't know why, your heart is racing, you argue with family members, avoid certain places or situations, and are always fighting the disturbing images that pop into your mind. When night comes, you can't sleep and are haunted by nightmares. Over time, your world starts to shrink; maybe you can't work, and it's hard to see friends. Living with the symptoms of PTSD takes the joy out of life, leaves no energy for relationships, and denies you a sense of peace. No wonder people with PTSD start to feel depressed.

Research confirms that depression is likely to develop after a stressful life event. Stress hormones cause changes in the brain that not only contribute to the PTSD symptoms we've described, but also to depression. The cortisol system in particular seems to be operating abnormally in people with both PTSD and depression, leaving people with PTSD at higher risk for depression.

People often think that being depressed means you are sad or crying most of the time. It's actually just as common for depressed people to feel emotionally flat or numb, a symptom of both depression and PTSD. This is what Barry's depression looked like. When you are depressed, few things are fun, pleasurable, or fulfilling anymore, so you stop doing the things you once found enjoyable. People who are depressed also withdraw from others because they feel they are not good company, which leads to social isolation. Other symptoms of depression include difficulty sleeping, changes in appetite and eating, feeling tired (or sometimes agitated) during the day, trouble concentrating, a loss of interest in sex, and feelings of guilt or worthlessness.

While many of the skills and techniques of this book are helpful for both PTSD and depression, chapter 5 specifically focuses on pulling yourself out of the dumps, improving your mood, and reintroducing positive activities back into your life.

PTSD Coping Strategies That Don't Work

It's common for people with PTSD to look for ways to control their symptoms. Most of these coping strategies involve ways of reducing anxiety, which makes sense, but some coping strategies can actually intensify and perpetuate the problem. Understanding how unhelpful coping strategies such as avoidance and alcohol make things worse can help you replace them with strategies that do work, so you can overcome your PTSD.

Avoidance

Everyone who has experienced post-traumatic stress and anxiety engages in avoidance, one of the most common symptoms of PTSD as described above. It's only natural: If you find yourself becoming hyperalert and sweaty when you're around crowds, you stay away. If getting on buses or trains sets off your alarm system, you take your car instead. People learn very quickly that avoidance reduces their anxiety by dodging the cues or situations that trigger it.

Unfortunately, avoidance also trains your brain to see danger in more and more places, keeping your alarm system on high alert. It may relieve some of your anxiety in the short term, but it keeps PTSD alive for the long run. That's why avoidance is such a debilitating problem.

Fortunately, the ways to overcome avoidance (which we'll discuss in chapter 4) not only give you back your life, they literally rewire your brain to stop seeing threats around every corner. Learning to overcome avoidance behaviors is one of the most powerful tools you'll have for conquering post-traumatic stress disorder.

Alcohol and Drugs

Just like avoidance, alcohol and drugs reduce anxiety in the short term. Some people also use drugs or alcohol to recapture some of the positive feelings that are hard to find when you're struggling with PTSD and depression. But alcohol and drugs provide only temporary relief; they make PTSD symptoms worse and interfere with recovery in significant and important ways.

If using alcohol and drugs is one of the ways you cope, we encourage you to read chapter 7.

Withdrawing from Relationships

Many people who have experienced a trauma find that their relationships become strained. One of the reasons for this is a sense that others don't understand what it was like to experience your trauma or understand what you're still struggling with. Many people also find that as they feel increasingly alienated from their loved ones, they sometimes explode at them in anger. Conflict in your relationships makes you feel even more estranged and drives you to withdrawal even further.

It's therefore not uncommon for PTSD sufferers to shun family and friends. But this tendency to withdraw from social relationships makes things even harder: You don't have a good source of support and comfort, just when you need it the most. One of the key strategies for overcoming PTSD is reconnecting in healthy ways with others, the topic of chapters 8 and 9.

Moving Forward

Now that you are armed with a good understanding of PTSD, it's time to overcome the pain, fear, and negative symptoms that have been controlling your life. Right now you may feel trapped and helpless, but there are ways that you can feel safe and connected to this world again, building on your natural strengths and resilience. The rest of this book is dedicated to helping you develop the skills you need to conquer your symptoms in a healthy way, improve your relationships, and integrate your trauma experience into your life so you can grow and move forward.

SECTION 2

Overcoming Anxiety, Avoidance, and Depression

CHAPTER 3

Reduce Anxiety by Modifying Your Stress Responses

Ian

After the assault, Ian, the computer programmer who was mugged as he walked to his car after work (see page 20), wasn't surprised that he was a bit anxious. For the first few months he had a hard time whenever he approached the parking garage: he could feel his muscles tense and his breathing quicken as he got closer to his car. Six months later, Ian noticed that he was increasingly edgy and irritable at work. He would often watch strangers on elevators or on the street, looking for suspicious behavior. He could feel that his internal alarm system was always on ready alert. He couldn't concentrate at work; most nights he had trouble relaxing enough to fall asleep before 2:00 a.m. or 3:00 a.m. Instead of fading away over time, Ian's anxiety was slowly building. He felt like he was losing control of his life.

■

Nicole

Nicole's anxiety started during the abuse in her childhood (see page 16). When her parents tried to be affectionate with her, she would start to feel dizzy and light-headed. She recoiled from teachers or other adults when they took her hand to cross the street. Sometimes her heart would race so fast that things would start to feel unreal, and she would retreat to some quiet place and try to clear her head. In high school and college, she gradually became more comfortable with limited physical contact, but she kept friends at a distance with a tough exterior and blustery, sarcastic humor. Dating made her extremely anxious, and she started having panic attacks when things got romantic or flirtatious with guys. As an adult, Nicole sometimes had periods without severe anxiety or panic attacks, but she felt trapped by her constant low-level tension, edgy irritability, and need to feel vigilant around others. It was exhausting.

One of the most upsetting symptoms of post-traumatic stress disorder is chronic, elevated anxiety. Like Ian and Nicole, you probably struggle with a constant underlying feeling of tension, punctuated with bouts of intense anxiety or panic attacks. Overwhelmed by a trauma, your stress alarm system is now on constant alert for danger, and is frequently triggered by high levels of adrenaline and stress hormones. And because anxiety sometimes seems to come out of the blue, you may feel like you have no control over it. You have become a prisoner of your anxiety.

But you don't have to be. As we discussed in chapter 2, the first step in overcoming anxiety is to understand it in ways that take the fear out of the fear, allowing you to learn new skills to modify your anxiety response. The key is to remember that anxiety is triggered when your brain perceives a danger, real or not. You want your stress alarm system to respond to *real* threats. Unfortunately, after a trauma your brain frequently misinterprets harmless cues or events as dangerous, causing false alarms. While you can't control your body's conditioned response to trauma-related triggers, you can learn new skills to help you tolerate anxiety and reduce it, including:

- Understanding anxiety to quickly identify false alarms

- Using knowledge about anxiety to overcome the natural fear of the physical sensations associated with the alarm system response

- Learning mindfulness methods for riding out your anxiety

- Learning techniques for grounding yourself when you feel overwhelmed

- Learning relaxation techniques to calm your alarm system, including slow breathing, progressive relaxation, imagery, meditation, and prayer

All of these skills are well-established techniques in the effective treatment of anxiety. Like all skills, they are learned through practice. You can't just pull them out when you're anxious; you must practice them repeatedly or integrate them into your daily routine so they become natural, ingrained habits. Once you do, anxiety will no longer rule your life.

The anxiety scale on the next page is a tool to help you measure the level of your anxiety, fear, or distress at any given moment. Consult this scale before and after any of the exercises, to see if the technique you're practicing helps to reduce your anxiety. Note that the physical symptoms of anxiety can occur at any level, but usually increase in number and intensity as anxiety increases. These symptoms include: increased heart rate, sweating, trembling or shaking, feeling dizzy, light-headed or faint, sweating, shortness of breath or choking sensations, chest pain, nausea or abdominal distress.

Rating	Severity	Description: You feel . . .
0	none	No distress or anxiety: absolutely calm and relaxed.
1	minimal	Mostly calm, but have a twinge of tension or alertness that isn't very noticeable.
2	mild	Slightly tense or nervous, but are still able to focus on your work or social activities.
3	mild	Mildly stressed, tense, or nervous. You can work or social-ize but you have to actively manage the anxiety, and you may be irritable. Your body may be tense or "keyed up."
4	moderate	Mild-to-moderate anxiety, and somewhat distracted or irritable. You have mild physical symptoms such as muscle tension or feeling weak or shaky.
5	moderate	Moderately anxious and/or stressed, interfering somewhat with your ability to focus or work; distracted, hyperalert, and on guard. Physical symptoms may include increased heart rate, light-headedness, butterflies, irregular breathing.
6	moderate	Very anxious, distracted, hypervigilant. You may feel dizzy, light-headed or shaky, with rapid heart rate, tightness in the chest, nausea, etc.
7	severe	Intensely anxious and/or distressed, with strong physical symptoms. You have difficulty concentrating on any-thing but the anxiety.
8	severe	Very intense and overwhelming anxiety, with significant physical symptoms (pounding heart, rapid breathing, sweating, dizziness, nausea). You are focused on want-ing to get out of the situation.
9	extreme	Extreme fear and distress and significant difficulty coping. Physical sensations are intense and you are entirely focused on escaping the situation.
10	extreme	Panic and fear you may die, faint, or lose your mind. Your fear is so intense you are overwhelmed and can only think of escape.

Reduce Anxiety by Modifying Your Stress Responses   **47**

Skill 1

Recognizing False Alarms

As we discussed in chapter 2, your stress alarm system can be triggered by any threat, real or false. If you're out on a country walk and think you spot a rattlesnake, that's a real threat that will set off a strong alarm response. But if the "snake" turns out to be a curved stick, what you've just experienced is a false alarm.

People with PTSD or other anxiety disorders experience frequent false alarms. Following a trauma, your brain interprets many different kinds of situations and cues as dangerous, even though they are actually harmless. These triggers are usually similar to the original traumatic event, though new triggers can also develop over time and cause your alarm system to be tripped over and over. It usually starts with a sight, sound, or smell that reaches your senses. For instance, if Ian sees several strangers huddling on a street corner as he walks to his apartment in the evening, his brain instantly thinks *Threat!* and throws the stress alarm switch. Before he's even had time to register that he is afraid, he's crossed the street, his heart racing. By the time Ian has reached the other side, he's seen that the strangers are merely a neighbor and his sons, whose presence has triggered a false alarm.

Sometimes the trigger isn't obvious. In Nicole's case, she found herself becoming anxious as she sat in a local café, reading the paper. Eventually, she stopped going to the cafe. Years later in therapy, she realized that the smell of coffee was the trigger: Her uncle drank a lot of coffee, and her brain made that association, setting off a warning alarm.

Your brain is designed to sense cues associated with the trauma and set off an alarm response, even when you aren't aware of it, and even when the danger is no longer present. The first skill for managing your anxiety is to recognize these false alarms, and to challenge your natural response to the anxiety they produce.

Recognizing False Alarms

1. When you notice you are anxious, look around and figure out what has triggered your alarm system.

2. When you have identified the trigger (strangers on the corner), determine what you think the threat is (they intend to mug me).

3. Determine if there really is a danger present, or if you've just experienced a false alarm (I know those people—it's my neighbor and his sons).

4. Say to yourself: "This danger isn't real. This is a false alarm."

5. Go easy on yourself: Anxiety responses after a trauma are natural.

It's important to know that your alarm system plays an important role—if there were a fire, you would want to have all that physiological juice helping you to respond to the emergency. If the Houston bay was starting to surge during a heavy storm, you'd want your alarm system working and motivating you to get to higher ground. But in the case of false alarms, you want to be able to turn your alarm system off. When you make a conscious effort to recognize that your stress alarm system is responding to a trauma trigger (and not a real danger), you can identify false alarms and quickly bring down your anxiety.

Skill 2

Remind Yourself That Alarm Sensations are Harmless

Most people find anxiety and the physical symptoms of their stress alarm systems very disturbing, especially when they arise unexpectedly. Heart racing, dizziness, flushed face, shaky hands, chest pain—these symptoms can make you feel like you are going to have a heart attack or faint. The intense sense of fear and panic can also make you afraid that you are losing control or "going crazy." And so the anxiety symptoms trigger more anxiety. It's a spiral that can keep going up, sometimes escalating into a panic attack. You can stop this escalating spiral by reminding yourself that *the sensations of the alarm symptoms going off are harmless.*

To do this, you need to remind yourself how the normal stress alarm system works. You may recall from chapter 2 that the physical symptoms of anxiety are part of a normal, healthy response to stress; they may feel uncomfortable but they are not dangerous. The physiological changes are designed to boost oxygen and sugar levels in your blood for energy, and to quickly direct blood to your muscles for action.

Let's consider some common fears people have about the physical sensations of anxiety:

- "I'm having a heart attack." Your heart starts pounding when you are anxious, in order to increase circulation.

You may also have tension or pain in your chest because your chest muscles tighten to increase breathing. These changes are totally different from a heart attack, which involves blockage of a heart vessel.

- "I'm going to faint." You may feel this way because increased breathing (hyperventilation) causes higher levels of oxygen relative to carbon dioxide in your blood. This shifts your blood pH to become more alkaline, which makes you feel light-headed, dizzy, and weak. But these changes, while uncomfortable, will not cause you to faint—in fact, anxiety slightly raises blood pressure to ensure that you do not.

- "I'm going to lose control." This fear arises because stress hormones cause intense physical changes in your body that create a strong need to escape. The truth is, your mind is actually sharpening to assess the threat, and your body is getting ready to fight or flee. You are actually very focused and prepared. When people are anxious, they do not lose control; they handle themselves pretty well despite feeling frightened.

- "I'm losing my mind." While anxiety can be overwhelming, you are not losing your mind or becoming psychotic. Psychotic disorders such as schizophrenia are largely genetic and develop in late adolescence: If you were going to develop it, chances are you already would have well before the trauma.

So whether the threat that is triggering your alarm system is real or not, remind yourself again that the alarm system response itself is not dangerous.

Alarms Sensations Are Harmless

1. Notice when you're anxious and your alarm system causes physical sensations, such as increased heart rate, sweating, trembling or shaking, feeling dizzy, light-headed or faint, sweating, shortness of breath or choking sensations, chest pain, nausea or abdominal distress.

2. Remind yourself: "These sensations are only my stress alarm system going off, and they are not dangerous."

3. Repeat additional coping statements to yourself, such as the ones below or ones you've made up for yourself:

   - "The sensations of anxiety are uncomfortable, but not dangerous."

   - "This is just a false alarm."

   - "These sensations won't hurt me."

Skill 3

Riding Out the Anxiety

Anxiety does not go on forever: It always comes down. Your body cannot sustain the alarm response for very long—it takes a lot of stress hormones and energy to keep the system in high gear. The alarm system is also designed to be short-lived, shutting off quickly as the threat passes. First, you'll notice your heart rate and breathing calm down after a few minutes, as the fast adrenalin system turns off. Then, over the next 10 to 45 minutes, the slower cortisol system that provides sustained energy goes back to baseline. These systems are not built to keep your anxiety high for a long period unless the danger persists.

One of the most powerful tools at your disposal is simply to ride out the anxiety like it's a rollercoaster—scary, but lasting only a few minutes. Don't fight it, don't try to escape it, just notice the anxiety and let it be. Observing and accepting your emotion in the moment is called "mindfulness." You can also use some of the relaxation techniques described later in the chapter, such as slow breathing. Remind yourself it is only a false alarm, and that the symptoms are harmless and will end soon.

Here's how Ian coped:

> When I'd see some guys hanging out on the corner, I'd notice my anxiety go to an eight—pretty intense. I'd feel that thump-thump in my chest, and it felt like I couldn't catch my breath. My body would tense up and my hands would get clammy. I used to turn around right then or cross the street, but I began to stop when this happened, to stay where I was. My anxiety would stay at a seven or eight for about two minutes, but I kept telling myself to wait. And sure enough, after a few minutes I could feel the anxiety start to drop to a three or four, and my breathing slow. I'd pretend to be looking at my phone as I stood on the sidewalk, and wait another minute. Then I'd continue walking.

Staying with the anxiety takes tremendous strength and courage—you actually have to resist the sirens going off in your brain. But if you can hang in there for a few minutes, you will quickly learn that your anxiety level will drop. You can handle it. If you leave the situation when you are suddenly anxious, however, you reinforce the fear. Your behavior tells your brain that the situation was indeed dangerous. You need to give it another message:

Nothing bad will happen if you stay. Every time you ride out the anxiety, the next time will be easier.

Skill 3 Practice

Riding Out the Anxiety

1. When you notice you are anxious, tell yourself calmly: "Ride it out."

2. Stay where you are, and wait for a few minutes.

3. Count to ten, breathe slowly, look out the window, stretch; imagine a peaceful, calm place.

4. Rate your anxiety (0–10); be aware as your anxiety level decreases.

5. Don't fight the anxiety, just observe it and let it be.

6. Tell yourself:

   - "Don't fight the anxiety, just let it pass."

   - "Anxiety does not go on forever. Wait it out."

   - "I will survive this anxiety, just as I have before."

Skill 4

Grounding Yourself

After a traumatic experience, you can sometimes become overwhelmed by uncontrollable fear or emotional pain, unable to stop thinking or imagining the event. These moments of intense anxiety and panic may make you feel as if you're having a flashback. For Nicole, moments of overwhelming anxiety triggered dissociation, a feeling of being strangely removed from herself and others, almost as if she were disappearing.

If this happens to you, grounding activities help you shift your attention and soothe the feeling. Grounding works by yanking your focus away from your inner turmoil and redirecting it to the outside world—the chair you're are sitting on, the view outside the window, cold water running on your hands. Grounding helps you gain control over your feelings, pulling you back into the present moment.

There are many ways to ground yourself. We've provided some suggestions below. As you look these over, you may realize that you already have your own grounding techniques. Use your own, try our suggestions, or make up new ways to bring yourself back to the present. It's helpful to include a self-statement that reminds you where you are, that this is the present and not the past, that you are safe.

SKILL 4 PRACTICE

Grounding

Focus on your immediate environment

- Wherever you are, stop and look around at the room or outdoor environment.

- Describe your environment in detail, out loud or to yourself. Take your time, do it thoroughly, keep your eyes moving. Inside, try describing colors, paintings, furniture and fixtures, objects on display, sounds, and textures. Outside, describe buildings, trees, items on display in shop windows, parks, smells, and sounds.

- Make a safety statement to yourself: "I am in the present, not the past." "That was then, this is now." "I am safe right now."

Focus on physical activity

- Run cold or hot water over your hands or face; hold an ice cube.

- Grab tightly onto a chair as hard as you can. Notice how your muscles tense.

- Do something physical to clear your head—stretch, jump, run, dance.

- Do a slow breathing exercise (see Skill 5), and focus on your breath.

- Carry something in your pocket that you can touch and describe to yourself (a paperclip, rock, marble) or a rubber band that you can snap.

- Remind yourself: "That was then, this is now." "I am safe right now."

Focus on mental distraction

- Out loud, list your favorite foods, animals, places to visit, members of a sports team, the words to a song, all fifty states.

- Remember the last joke or funny story that made you laugh.

- Imagine and remember in detail a favorite place (see Skill 7).

- Say to yourself: "I am in the present, not the past." "That was then, this is now." "I am safe right now."

Using Relaxation Techniques to Beat Anxiety

Relaxation techniques are also powerful tools for gaining control over anxiety. Learning to relax may seem next to impossible if you have PTSD, but it's actually much easier than you think. Just as our stress alarm system activates our bodies with adrenalin and other stress hormones to gear us up for action, we have a calming system that is designed to shut off the alarm response and soothe the mind and body. This system is also controlled by the brain, slowing down your heart rate and breathing, relaxing your muscles, reducing shaking and sweating, and bringing down your anxiety and vigilance levels so your body can return to its normal state.

Scientists have learned that we have the power to activate our calming systems ourselves, and research shows that people who regularly activate their calming systems with relaxation techniques have less stress and anxiety. You can do it, too.

As a first step, we recommend that you practice relaxation skills when you are not anxious. And don't try too hard to do it right—forcing yourself can actually make you more stressed and tense. For all of these relaxation exercises, take the pressure off by letting yourself relax instead of forcing yourself to relax. Don't work at trying to make the anxiety or tension go away. Just let it be. Let go of your need to be in control, then shift your attention to your breathing or to some positive image (read about imagery below). Experience whatever you are experiencing, then focus on relaxation; the tension will drift away naturally. Once you've mastered some of these relaxation techniques, use them when you become anxious to ride out your anxiety.

Slow Breathing

Did you know that different breathing patterns promote different emotional states? Your breathing rate naturally speeds up when you experience stress or anxiety. Muscles in your abdomen tighten up and your chest cavity is constricted, causing you to feel like you're suffocating when you "over-breathe" or hyperventilate. But you are not suffocating. Your increased breathing rate and the tightening in your chest are simply your body's attempts to bring in more oxygen. If you don't use that extra oxygen to fight or flee, though, it will cause the ratio of oxygen to carbon dioxide in the blood to shift, lowering your blood's pH level and making it more alkaline. This change is not bad for you, but it does cause some physical sensations that people find unpleasant, such as dizziness, weakness, tingling, and a dry mouth. Slowing down your breathing will return your pH to normal and allow your calming system to take over.

The slow breathing technique is very simple: Just focus on your breath and slow it down a bit. Become aware of your breathing, noticing how the air is cool as you bring it in and warm as you exhale. Don't force yourself to breathe in a way that feels pressured or unnatural. Think of it as a light touch, a slight slowing, which may be all you have to do to slow your breath. Some people like to count, breathing in for three seconds, and then out for three seconds. Many find that they exhale longer than they inhale, which is fine too. As you exhale, it's also nice to say something to yourself, like *calm* or *let go*. Do what works for you.

Slow breathing is sometimes called deep breathing, because as you slow your breath and start to relax, you start breathing from a deeper place, called abdominal breathing. Have you ever watched babies breathe while they sleep? Their stomachs, not their chests, rise and fall with their breath. When we are tense, though, we start breathing up high in our chests. After you slow your breathing, see if you can bring air into your belly, letting it rise; then slowly exhale and let your belly fall. If this seems too complicated or unnatural, don't do it. We don't want you to work too hard at this. Simply slow down and focus on your breath in a light, easy way, letting go.

As you begin to practice slow breathing, find a comfortable position, either reclining in a chair or lying on your back with your knees up. Later, when you get comfortable slowing your breathing, you'll find you can do it anywhere, anytime. Once you are in a relaxed position, close your eyes or gaze softly at the ground. You may hear sounds around you, and that is fine. You may notice thoughts popping into your head, and that's fine too. Don't resist anything—just notice the sound or thought and then let it go. You do not need silence to do any of these exercises.

SKILL 5 PRACTICE

Slow Breathing

1. Get into a relaxed position, and just notice your breathing.

2. See if you can lightly slow your breathing, just a little.

3. As you breathe out, say a relaxation word to yourself, like *calm* or *let go*.

4. Continue for several minutes.

Alternatively, you can try slow breathing with counting:

5. Get into a relaxed position, and notice your breathing.

6. Breathe in slowly as you count 1......2......3.....IN.

7. And let out your breath slowly 1......2......3.....OUT (*calm.....
let go*).

8. Continue for several minutes.

Skill 6

Relaxing Your Muscles

Your entire body tenses up when you are anxious. Learning to relax your muscles using progressive muscle relaxation (PMR) is a powerful way to reduce your stress or anxiety.

PMR involves squeezing and releasing different muscle groups in your body, working from your toes to your head. When you tense a muscle and hold it for ten seconds, you exhaust the muscle; when you release it, the muscle naturally becomes warmer, heavier, and more relaxed. We describe ways to tense certain muscles below, but if you find more effective ways of doing it, feel free to make those changes to the exercise. Keep in mind that as you do this exercise, you don't need to tense your muscles as hard as you can. Just try to tense them hard enough to make them shake slightly. If you have pain or a medical condition that would make it difficult to tense your muscles, don't do it; concentrate instead on relaxing them.

When you are ready to begin, find a comfortable position, either sitting up or lying down, and start by slowing your breathing. This exercise usually takes 20 to 30 minutes, so find a time once a day when you can practice without interruption.

Relaxing Your Muscles

Use this technique for each part of your body: Focus your attention on the specific part, and when you are ready, tense the muscles. For ten seconds, flex, squeeze, tighten, hold; then *relax* for ten seconds. Let your breath go, and direct your attention to the tension flowing out of the area, noticing how the muscles become warm, heavy, and loose. Breathe normally. Do this procedure in the following order, incorporating specific instructions that are given before you tense the muscles:

- Right foot: Lift your foot and curl your toes under.

- Right leg: Lift your leg off the floor; keep it straight and point your toes, so that you tighten your thigh muscles, knees, and calves.

- Left foot, then left leg: Repeat as for right.

- Abdomen: Tense the muscles around your stomach, hips, and lower back.

- Chest and upper back: Push your shoulder blades back (as if you were trying to have them touch) and tighten your chest.

- Right hand and arm: Hold your arm out in front, bend it toward you as if you're making a muscle, tense the muscles, and make a tight fist.

- Left hand and arm: Repeat as for right.

- Shoulders: Lift your shoulders, squeezing and tensing the muscles together into your neck.

- Neck: Drop your head forward, touching your chin to your chest, and tense all of your neck muscles.

- Face: Squeeze your eyes and mouth shut, pulling all the muscles into the center of your face.

After you've completed this exercise, mentally scan your body for any remaining tension, then focus on that muscle group, tensing and releasing as described. Once you are relaxed, enjoy the sensation. When you are ready, get up slowly.

SKILL 7
Using Imagery

Imagery, a relaxation technique that has gained popularity since the 1970s, involves visualizing yourself in a tranquil place that gives you a sense of calm and peace. For example, Nicole liked to imagine herself in a mountain meadow with the sun shining on her back, while Ian preferred to imagine himself on a beach, watching the waves gently roll in and out. Pick a place that you can visualize fully, perhaps a favorite vacation spot or a place you loved when you were a child. Imagining yourself there should make you feel warm, good, and safe. You can imagine a good friend or family member there with you, if it makes you feel more comfortable.

Mastering this technique means that you'll always be able to go to your safe place in your mind, whenever you feel anxious or afraid, and calm your fears.

Using Imagery

1. Begin to visualize the place you've selected. Imagine yourself arriving there, stretching out your arms and slowly taking in all the sights, sounds, and smells.

2. Visualize your peaceful surroundings in crisp detail. Watch the scene change as a bird lands on a branch or a sailboat drifts by. Let the scene soothe you.

3. What do you feel on your skin? Is it warm or cool? Is there a breeze? Feel the calm spread through your body as the sun caresses you.

4. Smell the pine trees, the scent of flowers, or the ocean breeze.

5. Imagine that you're lying back in the mountain meadow or strolling along the beach. You can move around in your place or relax into a comfortable position. Breathe.

6. Pick up a pinecone or handful of sand and feel the texture. Feel the ground crunch beneath you as you walk or lie down.

7. As you take everything in, let yourself fall into a state of deep relaxation and peace.

Skill 8

Using Meditation and Prayer

All over the world, people use meditation and prayer to comfort themselves, find inner peace, and connect with someone or something greater than themselves alone.

Many who are religious use prayer to cope when they face difficult situations or painful emotions. Prayer can remind you of your inner strength, your faith, and your belief in the goodness of others and the world. When you are anxious, prayer can be a powerful way to help you let go and put your trust in God or your Higher Power.

Meditation may be less familiar to you, but it can also bring similar feelings of peace. Many religions have traditions dating back thousands of years on the nature of meditation. It was not until late in the twentieth century, however, that the effects of meditation were thoroughly researched and found to be a very effective way to help people center and relax. Most types of meditation involve detaching from your thoughts and feelings, and focusing on a single word (mantra) or your breath. You don't try to stop your thoughts and feelings (you can't!), but rather, you simply notice them flow by and then return your attention to your breath. This is the concept of "mindfulness" discussed in skill 3: being aware of your thoughts and feelings, without resistance.

Both meditation and prayer can help you move beyond your day-to-day worries and concerns, in order to gain perspective and appreciate a wider consciousness. By detaching a little from your life and seeing yourself as but a small part of a greater whole, you can sometimes gain a little distance from the disturbing emotions left over from the trauma.

There are many good books on meditation and spiritual growth. You may want to consult your pastor, spiritual guide, or trusted friend for a recommendation about a book or a class to learn more.

Moving Forward

The techniques we've been talking about can only become part of your life through practice. We encourage you to try each of them out for a week, although over time you may settle on a few keepers that work especially well for you. It's especially important when you first try them out to practice when you are not anxious, so that you can really learn the skill well. Pick regular times during the day, perhaps in the morning and at bedtime, when you are going to practice. Write your practice schedule in your journal and keep to it. If you make these skills part of your daily routine, we believe you will feel the difference in your life.

CHAPTER 4

Overcoming Avoidance by Stepping Out

Dan

When Dan came back from Iraq, he found he didn't like being on the freeway. When trucks followed his car too closely, it reminded him of being in a convoy, and he felt like a target. He also became anxious and hypervigilant around crowds. He started to avoid activities he once loved, such as going to football games and rock concerts and had the same reaction in crowded stores, bars, or restaurants. Even drinking with buddies at a bar made him edgy if too many people started coming in: He'd find himself scanning the room, and his heart would start pumping if a stranger came too close. After about six months, he started staying closer to home and declining invitations from his friends. He asked his wife, Heather, to do the shopping, and when he had to run an errand or go to an appointment, he bolstered himself with a couple of shots of Jack Daniels.

■

Sonya

Sonya noticed that there were a number of situations she started to avoid after the accident. She couldn't drive because most of the bones in her left arm and hand were shattered, but when her physical therapist said she could learn to drive with one hand, she refused. The thought of driving terrified her. Even being a passenger in another person's car provoked intense anxiety. After she returned to work, Sonya reluctantly took the bus on days she had to go in, and spent the rest of her time telecommuting from home. Her avoidance of driving severely limited what she could do, and she felt trapped in her house. Sonya also found that she couldn't watch action movies with car chases on television anymore, and started turning off news programs, which seemed increasingly violent to her.

Trauma suddenly turns the world into a dangerous place. For people with PTSD, like Dan and Sonya, situations that remind them of the trauma trigger anxiety and avoidance. Many Vietnam veterans still find themselves cringing at the sound of helicopters and staying away from tropical vacation spots. Around such triggers, their brains still scream *Danger!* even though the danger is long gone.

Our brains are wired to learn that the things associated with a traumatic event predict danger and should be avoided. This tendency to become anxious in response to sights, sounds, places, and other cues associated with trauma is known as conditioning, a type of nonconscious learning that is designed to help us survive similar situations. Unfortunately, a "similar" place or activity may in fact not be dangerous at all. Once the danger of the trauma has passed the brain is slow to unlearn these associations. In fact, these triggers lead you to avoid more and more situations in your life, shrinking your world over time.

Fortunately, there is an effective process for overcoming conditioned fear and avoidance—the exposure technique. Learning this technique will help you retrain your brain to understand that the situations you fear are no longer dangerous for you. Exposure work does require courage and determination, but it is a tried-and-true method that will open up your world again.

In this chapter, we'll talk about conditioning—why it happens, how it leads to avoidance, and how avoidance snowballs to constrict your world. You'll identify the situations you avoid, then learn how to do exposures to reduce your anxiety and avoidance. You may want to do the following exercises in your notebook or journal.

What Triggers Your Avoidance?

If you have experienced a traumatic event, you have probably noticed that you avoid certain "cues" or situations. These are sights, sounds, smells, or places that remind you of the trauma experience. For Dan it was crowds, and for Sonya it was action movies and driving. Take a look at the table on the next page for additional examples of the particular cues that can trigger anxiety after different types of trauma—cues that people will try to avoid if possible.

Trauma	Situations or Cues That Trigger Anxiety
Almost drowning	Running water, baths, pools, the beach
Being mugged near car	Parking lots, dark enclosed spaces
Failing to rescue woman in fire	Barbecues, smoky kitchens, ladders, firehouse, the scent of perfume
Earthquake	Plane turbulence, rumbling from truck driving by
Combat in Iraq	Hot sunny day, groups of men on the street, lines of trucks on the highway
Near-fatal heart attack	Hospitals, chest pain, room where it occurred, doctors in white coats
Tornado	High winds, TV weather channel, plane turbulence
Childhood sexual abuse	Physical exams, room where it occurred, being touched by others, adult sexual intimacy

How Avoidance Expands Beyond Trauma Cues

Avoidance behaviors can increase over time, as the places and activities that initially triggered your anxiety slowly expand to include others beyond the original trauma cues. With your alarm system on constant alert and unexpected anxiety-causing moments arising, more and more situations feel potentially dangerous to you, especially those where you may feel trapped or can't make a quick escape. Soon, you avoid riding on the subway, bus, or plane, sitting in the middle row at the movies, driving across a bridge, or getting stuck in a crowd. You may find that you cannot travel far from home or to unfamiliar places. You may no longer be able to stay alone, needing a relative or friend with you all the time. Often, people find the physical symptoms that occur during stress or anxiety—rapid heart rate or breathing, sweating, nausea, light-headedness—trigger even more anxiety, so they avoid stimulating activities such as exercise, hot baths, caffeine, or scary movies.

As years go by, avoidance becomes such an ingrained part of your life that it's hard to spot. Below are some of the common situations that people with PTSD often grow to avoid over time, no matter what type of trauma they have experienced:

- Public transportation (buses, trains, subway)

- Driving on bridges, through tunnels

- Crowded stores, clubs, movie theaters, or restaurants

- Long lines, busy roads, or freeways

- Traveling to unknown towns, neighborhoods, or far from home

- Taking unfamiliar routes to work, church, stores

- Social events that would be hard to leave (dinner party, sports event)

- Social events where you might get anxious

- Physically stimulating activities that cause physical symptoms (vigorous exercise, whirlpools, caffeinated drinks such as coffee and sodas)

Some of these situations you can easily avoid (for instance, taking the subway); other triggers you can't (as when a car backfires). What triggers your avoidance?

How Fear and Avoidance Develop: Conditioning

How do these trauma-related cues become triggers for your anxiety?
And why do they continue to trigger anxiety when you are no longer
in danger—often for months, even years, after the trauma? The
answer is conditioning, and understanding how it works will help
you change this automatic response.

Deep inside your brain is the fear center, called the amygdala
(ah MIG dah lah), which is designed to learn that anything associated with a stressful or traumatic experience predicts danger. The
amygdala is part of the older, "primitive brain," and it is essential to
survival. During a trauma or very stressful event, the amygdala
records details about the situation—sights, sounds, smells, locations. The next time you're in a similar situation, it will set off your
alarm system to prepare you for the anticipated danger. This very
adaptive system helped soldiers such as Dan learn without effort,
and after only one close call, that a truck on a highway in Iraq often
signals an attack. Troops in a war zone may not even be consciously
aware of any danger before their brains signal the threat by causing

their hearts to pound and their anxiety to surge. When this happens, they are instantly ready for action.

It was snowing when Sonya had her car accident, and she was drinking hot chocolate before she lost control of her car. In that moment of panic and terror, her amygdala recorded all of the associated details—snow, cold, cloudy sky, smell of chocolate, the news playing on the radio—with the danger. Her brain will continue to hold on to these perceived danger cues and trip her alarm system whenever she encounters them again.

It's important to understand that the amygdala isn't easily persuaded by reason or logic. It learns to respond to trauma cues automatically, whether the danger is real or imagined. That's why Sonya may rationally know she is safe in her house when it begins to snow outside, yet still have a strong anxiety reaction. Dan knows logically that he is in no danger of being blown up when he drives on the Texas highways, yet his amygdala still sets off false alarms whenever he gets in the middle of a row of trucks.

The problem with conditioning is that the brain is very slow to unlearn conditioned responses, even though the danger has passed. This occurs because from the amygdala's survival perspective, it's better to be safe than sorry. *Conditioning persists unless your brain actively learns that the cue no longer signals danger.* That's why people continue to have false alarms for a long time after a trauma.

Conditioning not only persists, it also expands, which explains why people with PTSD start avoiding more and more places and activities. Because the alarm system is stuck in overdrive after a trauma, the amygdala is primed to condition to new cues and situations.

For instance, Dan and his wife, Heather, sometimes went to the movies together. Initially, his brain didn't associate this activity with combat. But one day, after they took their seats in the almost empty theater, people started streaming in. Suddenly, the theater was packed. When the lights dimmed, Dan could feel people pressing in, trapping him. His anxiety level spiked. After several minutes of sitting there with his heart pounding and perspiration pouring down his face, Dan insisted that they leave. Because of the anxiety attack, Dan's amygdala now associated movie theaters with danger. The next time he went to a movie, he felt anxious even before he walked in.

Because your alarm system is on ready alert and easily triggers anxiety, you might find yourself developing fear responses in all kinds of situations. It's not a conscious process, and it's not one you can simply turn off. As the process continues, your world shrinks as you start to avoid more and more places.

The Good News: You Can "Unlearn" Conditioning

While your amygdala may not listen to reason, there is a way to retrain your amygdala to overcome conditioning. Just as your brain is designed to associate certain sights, sounds, and locations with danger, it is also equipped to unlearn those associations. You can teach your amygdala to stop responding to trauma cues with false alarms.

The process is called exposure, and here's how it works. You need to put yourself in the situation that is triggering anxiety, and wait long enough for your amygdala to see that the situation is no longer dangerous. If you repeatedly experience the feared situation or cue (driving in the snow, going into a crowded store or movie theater) without anything harmful happening, your amygdala will learn over time that the cue no longer signals danger. The association between the cue and danger is broken. This is how you "unlearn" conditioning. This exposure technique has been confirmed in thousands of studies on animals and humans as the primary way to retrain the amygdala to unlearn a conditioned fear response, and is highly effective in treating PTSD.

Why don't people naturally decondition without help? Because they either leave the situations that trigger their alarm systems, or avoid the places or activity altogether. But to retrain your amygdala, you have to stay in the situation long enough for your anxiety level to come down. Your brain has to learn that the movie theater or car is no longer dangerous, and it can only do that if you remain there. If you flee or avoid, your conditioned fear not only persists, it gets stronger. To overcome anxiety, you have to face your fear, repeatedly.

Facing Your Fears—The Way Back to Life!

You may be thinking that you don't really *want* to face your fears. Many people with PTSD feel that the avoidance is worth it. When you avoid places, situations, and memories that trigger your anxiety, you obviously keep your anxiety level lower. Or when you leave a situation that is triggering your alarm system, your anxiety goes down in that moment, which feels like a tremendous relief. Your escape behavior is instantly rewarded.

The rewards are short-lived, though. Avoidance is a strategy to manage anxiety in the moment, but it maintains your anxiety in the long run. That's why people who have PTSD or other anxiety disorders have trouble recovering from trauma on their own. The only way your brain can unlearn a conditioned response is for you to put yourself in the feared situation repeatedly, so your amygdala can break the association and learn that it is no longer dangerous. With exposure, you do this in a controlled, structured way. But if you keep avoiding situations that trigger anxiety, your brain will continue to think the cues truly are dangerous, and will keep issuing false alarms. Over time, conditioned fears and avoidance slowly strip away your freedom, spontaneity, joy, and sense of safety.

But it's quite possible to reverse the pattern. In the next section, we'll help you design some simple exposure exercises to decondition your amygdala and get you stepping out.

Exposure: Overcoming Fear and Avoidance

The exposure technique introduced here is backed by decades of research on how to reduce anxiety and avoidance. You must, however, learn the procedure accurately for it to be effective. You can do that by following the steps described in this chapter, or by working with a therapist trained in some form of exposure therapy. Dan and Sonya will be our guides through the process.

Basic Principles of Exposure Exercises

1. Put yourself in the situation that is triggering your anxiety.

2. Stay in the situation for at least 20 to 30 minutes. Your anxiety will peak for the first few minutes, then drop and level off.

3. Repeat this exposure four or five times or until your *starting* anxiety is very low, at 2 or 3.

Coping Skills to Use During Exposure Exercise

Because your anxiety level will increase during the exposure, it will be helpful to use several of the anxiety management techniques introduced in chapter 3. Before you begin the exposure exercises, review skills 2, 3, 4, and 5 (pages 52–60) to refresh your memory about these valuable coping techniques:

- Skill 2 will remind you not to fear the unpleasant physical sensations that accompany anxiety.

- Skill 3 will show you how to ride out the anxiety.

- Skill 4 provides grounding techniques to focus on the present.

- Skill 5 teaches you how to do slow breathing to calm yourself.

You will also want to refer to the Anxiety Scale on page 47.

Step 1: Create Your Avoidance List

Refer to page 71 and the list of cues and situations you try to avoid (in your journal). Make sure your list includes all of the places, activities, people, and situations you avoid since your trauma. Once your list is complete, imagine yourself in each situation, and, referring to the anxiety scale on page 47, rank your anxiety from 1 to 10 as if you were in that situation. To help you evaluate your anxiety levels, here are Sonya's and Dan's lists:

Sonya's List

Avoidance cues/situations	Anxiety Rating
Being a passenger in a car	5
Driving a car	9
Being on a bus	3
Walking near a busy intersection	5

Eating chocolate	4
Being out in snow or icy conditions	7
Watching the news (stories about accidents)	4
Watching action movies	8

Dan's List

Avoidance cues/situations	*Anxiety Rating*
Crowded sports events or big concerts	8
Crowded restaurants, bars	4
Driving an unfamiliar route to work or an appointment	7
Shopping malls on the weekend	6
Being outside in the sun when it's hot	3
Movie theaters	4
Being on the freeway with trucks in front and behind	9

Step 2: Pick a Situation on Your List

As you review your avoidance list, you'll notice that various situations trigger different levels of anxiety; they also have different degrees of importance in your life. For Sonya, not driving had a huge impact on her ability to do much of anything other than work or stay at home. Not eating chocolate or watching action movies, though, wasn't a big deal to her. Dan's anxiety around crowds really limited his activities, too; while he hadn't attended many football games, he did like to hang with friends at his favorite sports bar and take his wife to dinner.

Pick a situation or activity that you really want to be able to do, starting with one that has an anxiety rating in the low to moderate range (3 to 5 on the anxiety scale). Go through the exposure procedure with that item on your list. Once your anxiety has gone down significantly into the 1 to 2 range, you can move on to another situation.

Because Sonya wanted eventually to be able to drive, she picked for her situation being a passenger in a car, which she rated 5 on her anxiety scale. She was required to ride the bus to work everyday (a 3 rating), so in a sense she had already begun this exposure—and had noticed that it got easier with time. For his exposure, Dan picked going to a restaurant, which he rated 4.

Step 3: Design a Gradual Exposure

How do you teach a child to swim if he's afraid of water? Gradually. First, you might take him to the pool a few times, and just hang out and watch the other kids. Then you might have him stand near the pool for periods of five to ten minutes, until he seems comfortable being close to the water. Next, you could sit with him at the pool's edge, dangling both your feet in the water for ten minutes; then have him wear a life jacket in the shallow end of the pool, and so on. Each time, you repeat the exposure until the child's anxiety goes down, one step at a time.

Below are the plans that Sonya and Dan designed. Use these examples to design your exposure for the situation you selected.

Sonya: "Passenger in a car" gradual exposure

1. Sit inside a parked car

2. Have someone drive her around the block

3. Have someone drive her around the neighborhood (20 minutes)

4. Have someone drive her on the freeway (20–30 minutes)

Dan: "Crowded restaurant" gradual exposure

1. Go out to dinner early (5:00 p.m.) before it's too busy

2. Go out to dinner early (6:00 p.m.) when it's about half full

3. Go to popular restaurant at peak dinner hour when it's crowded

Design your gradual exposure plan in your journal.

Step 4: Do the First Exposure

Sonya and Dan are ready to begin the first steps of their exposures. They will rate their anxiety every few minutes during the exposure, so they can see their anxiety go down and track their progress over repeated exposures. They will also use anxiety-managing techniques from chapter 3 to calm themselves and ride out the anxiety. Afterwards, they'll reward themselves with a small pleasure—for Sonya, it's a bubble bath; for Dan, it's a basketball game on television.

Figure out what reward you'll give yourself, then follow this procedure for your exposure:

1. Select a day or time when you have adequate time—don't squeeze this in between commitments.

2. Have a friend or family member with you, if you want the support.

3. Put yourself in the situation.

4. Stay for a minimum of 20 to 30 minutes.

5. Rate your anxiety (mentally or on paper) every few minutes, using the anxiety scale on page 47.

6. Use coping skills to help you get through it (breathing, grounding, riding it out).

7. When you are finished with the exposure, write down what your anxiety levels were along the way. You at least want to record your starting level, peak level, and what it was at the end while you were still in the situation.

8. Congratulate yourself for your courage, and reward yourself with something soothing or pleasurable!

Step 5: Repeat Exposure Until Anxiety Is Low

To retrain your amygdala, you will need to repeat this exact exposure at least four to six times, until your anxiety in the first minutes of the exposure—which is generally your peak anxiety—is at a new low of 2 or 3. For Dan, this might mean going to an uncrowded restaurant twice a week for two weeks, until he's ready to move on to the next exposure. For Sonya, it might mean sitting in her car for 20 minutes, twice a day, for a week.

Step 6: Repeat Process with Next Level of Exposure

When Dan and Sonya found that their anxiety levels were fairly low, they moved on to their next exposures. For Dan, this meant going to a restaurant when it was somewhat crowded, and repeating this until his starting anxiety was a 2 or 3, which took him almost a month. Sonya asked her friend Laura, who knew about Sonya's fear of driving and was eager to help, to come over several times a week to do the exposure with her. Laura came over after work and drove Sonya around the block slowly several times. Afterwards, they sat inside to visit for a while. The friends did this for three weeks before Sonya was ready to move to the next exposure and have Laura take her on a longer drive around the neighborhood.

Moving to a Different Situation

Once you have worked through the gradual exposure list for the situation you targeted and your anxiety never goes above 2 or 3, you're ready to pick a different situation on your list. For example, once Sonya was able to let Laura drive her on the highway and anywhere around town, she decided that she wanted to tackle her most feared situation: driving herself. She again made a list of how she could do this gradually, starting with driving around the block repeatedly, and then slowly driving farther and farther from her house.

Dan picked the movie theater as the next situation to confront on his avoidance list. He structured it so that he and Heather would move closer to the center rows (and farther from the exit) each time they went. His starting anxiety in his first movie exposure was not as high as he had predicted, because his crowded restaurant exposures had already reduced his fear of other crowded situations. This is known as the generalizing or spreading effect of exposure: Reducing fear in one type of situation reduces it in similar situations.

People also Avoid Trauma Memories

As you attempt to stay in anxiety-provoking situations, you may find that more memories of the trauma start surfacing. Just as you have avoided situations that remind you of the trauma, you've also avoided memories of the trauma. Trying to avoid memories actually maintains their high degree of distress, causing them to intrude upon your day in images and thoughts that you can't control.

We'll talk about this in chapter 12 and provide techniques for working through your trauma memories. The process is similar to exposure therapy, because it requires you to confront something that causes you anxiety, as you work to decondition your fear of the memories. But the procedure is somewhat different from what is described above, and deserves its own chapter.

Moving Forward

It's important to take some time to recognize that the work you've been doing in this chapter takes tremendous courage. When you are struggling with PTSD, every cell in your body is crying out to escape or avoid anxiety-provoking situations. It takes great strength to resist the signals your alarm system is sending out, and put yourself in that anxiety situation on purpose—and stay! So take great pride in your exposure work, because it's a difficult road you've decided to travel. Be sure to plan a little reward for yourself with each new victory, every step of the way.

CHAPTER 5

Fight Depression by Challenging Negative Thinking and Getting Active

Barry

Like many trauma survivors, Barry, the firefighter who was unable to save the woman trapped in the fire, coped by shutting down (see page 18). A confident but quiet and stoic man, Barry naturally responded to his anxiety and gnawing guilt by withdrawing into himself. He walked around the house expressionless; he watched a little television, but rarely seemed interested in going out with his kids or having friends over for a barbecue. His wife, Shaundra, noticed his flat, joyless manner and his trouble sleeping through the night, but did not recognize them as signs of depression. She struggled with how distant he was, but figured he needed the space. It was his more obvious PTSD symptoms—being easily startled, avoidance, nightmares—that brought him into the clinic for an assessment. At that point he was also diagnosed with depression, a surprise to both Barry and his wife.

Angela

Initially, Angela's depression looked like normal grief, but it lasted much longer (see page 19). After holding services for her mother who died in Hurricane Katrina and moving to Houston to live with her sister, she was deeply distraught in the first few months. Besides struggling with PTSD symptoms, she found herself crying almost every day, plagued with guilt and insomnia; she lost 20 pounds. When the pain and despair continued for half a year, Angela knew that her grief had taken on a life of its own. Trying to establish herself in Houston was an overwhelming task, and she often woke up in a dark mood and had trouble getting out of bed. Eventually, she got a job as a receptionist, but she started missing work because of her fatigue, increasing panic attacks, and plummeting self-confidence. She was fired from two jobs for taking too much time off, and went on unemployment. She spent most of her time in the house, never making friends or getting to know her new community.

Depression is a natural response to the prolonged stress and grief that often follow a trauma. It takes a lot of energy to function when the world does not feel safe and every day is an internal fight with anxiety. It takes even more energy if you are coping with a significant loss. The chronic stress of PTSD tends to wear you down and rob you of any zest for life. Your mind and brain go into survival mode and you focus on avoiding threat, anxiety, and conflicts. Somewhere along the way, you start to see everything in a negative light. Perhaps you can't remember what it was like to have fun or to genuinely laugh. Because of these changes, you may withdraw from others and stop doing the things you once loved to do. Unfortunately, this only makes matters worse, reinforcing the sense of isolation and joylessness.

This chapter will describe how you can pull out of this downward spiral, which often leads to situational depression in people with PTSD. The first step involves recognizing how depression alters your mind to see things in a critical, self-blaming, and hopeless light; then, you'll learn techniques for assessing and revising your negative interpretations, which will quickly improve your mood. Finally, we'll illustrate some powerful exercises to get you engaged again with your family, community, and work. These "behavioral activation techniques" have been shown in research to be one of the most effective ways to combat depression and revive a positive sense of self. Whether you are depressed or not, these techniques can bring back the vitality and well-being that are frequently lost following a trauma.

Recognizing Depression

Symptoms of depression are very common among people suffering from PTSD. You may have noticed that you've been feeling very down for a while or that you have no motivation to work. Maybe life just feels harder, and the future looks bleak. You may recognize these feelings of sadness, hopelessness, or low motivation and energy as signs of depression. But few people know that depression affects your entire body and mind. It disrupts your normal patterns of sleeping and eating, often causing significant weight change and insomnia. Sometimes people feel increased irritability and anger instead of sadness—you find yourself overreacting to what coworkers say, or blowing up at home. At other times, people become emotionally flat, like Barry. Depression can rob you of any sense of pleasure or enjoyment in life. Depression also changes the way you think about yourself and the world, casting a dark, negative light on everything. You keep feeling that you are failing, that others are judging you. Suicidal thoughts are common, although most people do not act on them. Depression commonly leads to difficulties working, going to school, or even taking care of daily tasks.

The good news is that there are successful ways to reduce depression. They include techniques described here, as well as professional treatments for depression (see box on page 88). Are you experiencing any depression? Check this list of symptoms:

Signs of Depression

Physical symptoms

- Fatigue, exhaustion

- Low energy

- Change in appetite, or weight loss or gain

- Trouble falling asleep, frequent waking, or sleeping too much

Mood symptoms

- Feeling down, sad or blue

- Feeling emotionally flat

- Irritability or anger

- Tearfulness or frequent crying

- Feeling worthless; low self-esteem

- Feeling guilty or ashamed

Effect on thinking

- Negative, catastrophic thinking

- Dark or bleak sense of the future

- Critical, blaming thoughts (toward self and/or others)

- Suicidal thoughts

Effect on attention and memory

- Difficulty concentrating

- Difficulty maintaining attention

- Memory problems

Motivational symptoms

- Low sex drive

- Loss of interest or pleasure in activities

- Bored or unmotivated

- Wanting to return to or remain in bed

Social and/or occupational impairment

- Drop in performance at work or school

- Unemployment or underemployment

- Withdrawal from current relationships

- Lack of conversation with people you meet

When to Seek Professional Help

If you are experiencing any of the depression symptoms described, you should consider seeking professional care from a psychiatrist, psychologist, or other mental health professional. There are many effective treatments for depression, including antidepressant medication, cognitive-behavioral therapy, interpersonal therapy, and many other therapeutic approaches. If you were recently thinking about suicide, call your local mental health center for an appointment; if you are actively thinking about it, call 911 immediately. There is much help they can provide you.

Traumatic Grief

Traumas such as natural disasters, car accidents, and military combat often involve not only life-threatening trauma to the survivor, but also the injury or death of people the survivor knew. If your trauma, like Angela's, involved a death or loss, then you are probably struggling not only with depression but also with what is called traumatic grief. Grieving is a response to loss, but the grieving process is often more intense or prolonged if the loss occurred as part of a traumatic event. Mourning a traumatic loss can be especially difficult when you throw PTSD and depression symptoms into the mix, but it should not be neglected.

Because working through traumatic grief is an important part of your recovery, we have dedicated a portion of chapter 13 to this topic. If you experienced a significant loss through trauma, we recommend that you start with this chapter on depression as a way to quickly improve your mood, enlarge your effective coping strategies and focus more specifically on your loss. There are also many excellent books written specifically on the subject of traumatic grief and coping with the death of a loved one.

Skills to Fight the Downward Spiral of Depression

Depression has a way of feeding on itself, causing you to think in negative ways that increase feelings of sadness, guilt, anger, and hopelessness. Depression also robs you of energy and motivation, so that slowly you stop engaging in activities that used to bring you pleasure. Because depression also erodes confidence and self-esteem, you start to withdraw from your relationships, further reducing the very social contact and support that you need when you're depressed.

The key to overcoming depression is to break this spiral by challenging the way it makes you think and re-engaging others and the world. In this chapter, we'll give you the skills to:

- Gain perspective to overcome hopelessness.

- Challenge your pessimistic thinking to counteract negative feelings.

- Increase positive feelings through scheduling pleasurable, fulfilling, and social activities.

- Lift depression by getting more exercise.

- Improve your mood by getting more light.

It is also very important to take care of your body when you are depressed. In addition to adding exercise to your routine, it's crucial to improve your eating and sleeping habits, and to resist the temptation to use alcohol or drugs to mask your symptoms. We'll talk about these topics in the next section.

SKILL 1

Gain Perspective to Overcome Hopelessness

Many people do not realize that depression causes a change in the way they see themselves and the world. Depression colors everything in dark hues. You feel more critical of yourself and others, you interpret events negatively, and the future seems bleak. Depression makes you see the glass as half empty, and sometimes completely empty. You can't imagine that you will ever feel better.

The important thing to understand is that these thoughts are actually *symptoms* of depression. The feeling of futility is influenced by depression's alteration of chemicals in your brain. These dark interpretations and forecasts are not true, even if they seem that way. Reminding yourself of this fact can really help you overcome your feelings of hopelessness. It is also the first step in making some changes that will help you see that the glass is at least half full.

SKILL 1 PRACTICE

Gain Perspective

1. Notice your thoughts as they turn dark or negative, or as you think that things will never be better and you will never feel better.

2. Remind yourself that your negative thoughts and feelings of hopelessness are *caused* by the depression.

---

3. Use these self-statements to gain perspective:

- "This negative thinking is a symptom of depression."

- "I am only thinking this way right now because of how depressed I feel."

- "Depression is making me misinterpret things negatively."

- "I will not always feel this way; things will be better in the future."

- "Most people with depression have gotten better and I eventually will too."

Challenge Your Negative Thinking to Fight Negative Feelings

The way you think about or interpret an event has a dramatic effect on how you feel emotionally. For instance, suppose you are at work, and a coworker walks by your desk and doesn't say hello. There are many ways you might interpret this event, and each generates a different emotional response in you:

Interpretation	Emotion
"She didn't see me."	neutral
"She's mad at me."	anxiety, anger
"She doesn't like me; no one at work likes me."	sadness
"She must be stressed about her sick child."	sympathy

When you are depressed, you will usually interpret situations in the most negative way, assuming that others are mad at you, don't like you, think you are incompetent, don't care about you, and so on. People make these types of interpretations *automatically*—more out of habit then careful thought. Your interpretation or "automatic thought" then creates more painful feelings of sadness, anxiety, anger, worthlessness, incompetence, or guilt. You are in a vicious cycle: Depression causes negative thinking; negative thinking makes you feel worse.

You can fight this cycle by recognizing that these interpretations are really thinking errors that result from depression, then challenging them, and finally replacing them with a more realistic interpretation.

Step 1: Identify Your Thinking Error

There are a number of common thinking errors that have been identified for depression, though these errors are also commonly made when people are anxious or angry as well. Notice which errors you tend to make when things happen.

- **Black or white thinking.** This is the tendency to take one particular event or interaction, and use it to jump to global and extreme conclusions about yourself, others, or your work. When something happens, black-or-white thinkers put it in a category of all or nothing, good or bad, wonderful or rotten. For example, a friend cancels a coffee date, and you say to yourself, "She's mean," or "No one likes me anymore." You snap at your children one morning while you are rushing to go out and you say to yourself, "I'm a terrible parent," instead of the more balanced assessment: "I am someone who can be irritable sometimes." Black or white thinking will exaggerate any negative feeling, but especially those of sadness, hopelessness, anger, and guilt.

- **Taking it personally.** This is the tendency to be convinced that when someone hurts your feelings or upsets you, their actions were *intentional and directed toward you.* Instead of allowing for the possibility that a perceived slight may be unintended, you think the person *meant* to ignore, dismiss, or harm you. Someone doesn't return your email for a week (because he's busy or on vacation), and you think, "He's mad at me" or "I must not be important to him." You spouse snaps at you because she is tired and stressed, and you think, "She is sick of dealing with me." This error tends to generate feelings of anger, righteousness, or guilt and shame.

- **Catastrophizing.** If something goes wrong, you see it as the worst case scenario, or as a sign that a major catastrophe is on the way. You get into a fight with your spouse and you think divorce is right around the corner. If you don't do well on a test, you think you'll fail the class. Catastrophizing is the tendency to expect that things will get much worse in the future. This type of negative thinking reinforces feelings of fear and hopelessness.

- **Shoulds.** These are rigid or unrealistic expectations for yourself or others that set you or them up for failure. For example, you *should always* have lots of energy, work extra hard, or always be nice; you *should never* have lost your temper. While everyone has a code of ethics they try to live by, the error here is the lack of flexibility and understanding if you or others do not follow those principles 100 percent of the time. The expectation of perfection will generally cause you to feel guilty, disappointed, and angry. And when you apply these inflexible principles to what you have done in the past (I should have/I shouldn't have), you are simply beating yourself up for something you can't change. It may be that you have some regret, but you should also have some understanding and forgiveness for yourself.

- **Name-calling.** This is the tendency to stick a negative label onto yourself or others ("I'm a failure," "He's a jerk") when something goes wrong. This is a specific type of overgeneralization: You take one instance at work in which you didn't do well, and turn it into a complete character judgment. Or your spouse doesn't like to do dishes, so you conclude that she must be a slob by nature. Name-calling is a particularly harsh form of blaming, and people who are depressed usually direct it at themselves.

- **Mind reading.** You assume that you know what your coworkers, friends, or family members are thinking. During a staff meeting, your supervisor comments that everyone must work harder. You assume that all of your coworkers are thinking that *you* are the one who has not been carrying your load. Or your friend says he can't come over to watch the game and you think, "He's tired of how glum I've been." It's just as likely that the person may not be thinking of you at all, or may be thinking positive things about you. So don't assume!

- **Glass half empty.** This is the tendency to pay attention to the things that aren't working, instead of the things that are. Your focus is almost entirely on the negative part of the conversation, excluding or dismissing the positive. You clearly see how you are falling short at work, but you don't note your accomplishments. Neutral or ambiguous events are interpreted in a negative way (the glass is half empty), instead of in a positive light (the glass is half full) or with a balanced perspective (it's both!).

Depression and anxiety tend to distort our thinking in these ways. See if you can come up with several examples of your own.

Journal Exercise: Thought Table

Identify a recent interpretation you made during an interaction with someone, and write down the situation, your automatic thought, and the thinking error. We've included an example below. Create your own table in your journal.

Situation	Thought	Error
1. Friend cancels coffee date with you.	"She doesn't care about me."	Taking it personally.

The first step described above is simply to recognize when you are making one of these errors. The next step is to challenge your negative thought.

Step 2: Challenge Your Negative Thought with Evidence

Most of the battle against negative thinking involves slowing down, identifying your thought, and labeling the error using the list above. Usually if you succeed in labeling your thought ("OK, I'm doing that black or white thinking again."), you are well on your way to challenging it. But there is more you can do to test how realistic your automatic negative thought is.

Angela is someone who tends to catastrophize. When she lost her last job after moving to Houston, she thought, "I'll never work again." But if she understands her thinking error as catastrophizing, the possibility opens up that this may not be the only outcome. Now she can start to challenge the thought by gathering evidence. This is an objective process, where you consider the evidence for and against the thought. What evidence is there that Angela might never work again? The evidence in support of her prediction is that she has been fired several times, and unemployed for two years due to her PTSD and depression. Evidence against her pessimistic thought is that there are effective treatments for depression and PTSD that can reduce her anxiety, panic attacks, and avoidance, which would in turn enable her to work. Additional evidence is that most people with PTSD who stop working do return to work. Finally, she has been making progress in treatment, and can already see how she might pick up a part-time job. A summary of the evidence is shown in the following table:

Thought	Error	Evidence For	Evidence Against
"I'll never work again."	Catastrophizing	1. I've lost two jobs. 2. I've been unemployed for two years.	1. There are effective treatments for depression and PTSD. 2. Most people with depression and PTSD return to work. 3. I have been making progress on reducing my depression and PTSD symptoms. 4. I used to be a good worker and when I regain my energy, I can return to my former ability.

Let's take another example. Barry's anxiety attacks and avoidance of trauma triggers started to undermine his confidence, and with the added depression, he found himself uncomfortable with others and less assured at work. He began to withdraw from his family and fellow firefighters. These common symptoms of depression all came together in one painful thought that plagued Barry regularly: "I am weak."

What are the errors in Barry's thinking? His thought takes his current situation (avoidance and withdrawal due to PTSD and depression) and labels it in a black or white way as a character flaw (name calling). Barry could see the thinking error, but he wasn't convinced that his thought was extreme or distorted. So he reviewed the evidence. In support for his thought that he is "weak," Barry wrote down the fact that he had been avoiding places that triggered his anxiety, and that he felt less confident and comfortable with others. Evidence challenging his thought is that he did not engage in these behaviors before the trauma, and everyone with PTSD and depression initially engages in very similar kinds of avoidance and withdrawal. In other words, Barry's behavior is fairly normal given his situation. He is also showing great courage and perseverance in attempting to work on his symptoms.

CHALLENGING YOUR NEGATIVE THOUGHT (BARRY'S EXAMPLE)

Thought	Error	Evidence For	Evidence Against
"I'm weak."	Black/white thinking Name calling	1. I avoid places and gatherings where I might have anxiety. 2. I don't feel comfortable around others. 3. I'm not confident at work.	1. These are new behaviors for me (not my usual "character"). 2. Most people with PTSD and depression show these behaviors. 3. I am demonstrating my strength and courage by directly confronting and working on my PTSD and depression.

Now you can work on your own example in your journal. You just need to add one more column to the table:

Situation	Thought	Error	Evidence For	Evidence Against
1. Friend cancels coffee date.	"She doesn't care about me."	Taking it personally.	1. She cancelled the last time too. 2. We haven't spent much time together lately.	1. She's been calling and trying to get together. 2. She's been really busy at work. 3. She's been a committed friend for five years.

Step 3: Adopt a Realistic Thought

At this point it should be clear to both Angela and Barry that they need to revise their original interpretation to make their thoughts more realistic. A realistic thought resists the pull of thinking errors, and attempts to find a more balanced appraisal of the situation. Many of your negative thoughts have some grain of truth, and it's important to acknowledge this. For example, Angela's struggle with unemployment is real; so are Barry's shaken confidence and avoidance. But the thinking errors are biased to see only the negative and not the positive side, the alternative possibilities, the gray between the black and white. You don't have to pretend that the negative doesn't exist; just remember and acknowledge your strengths, successes, and progress in overcoming your difficulties.

What realistic thoughts could Angela and Barry could come up with?

Angela's Realistic Thoughts

- "I'm unemployed now, but I am working to reduce my symptoms so I can go back to work in the future."

- "Once my PTSD is better, I will be able to return to work."

- "Even if I still have PTSD, my new coping skills will enable me to work at least part-time in the future."

Barry's Realistic Thoughts

- "I may be struggling right now, but I'm fighting this PTSD and depression."

- "I'm not back to my old self yet, but I'm on my way back."

- "After going through this experience, I realize just how tough I am."

> **Journal Exercise: Thought Table with Realistic Thoughts**
>
> As you look over your own examples, what realistic thought
> can you come up with to replace your original thought?
> Add another column to your own table in your journal:
>
> | Situation | Thought | Error | Evidence For | Evidence Against | Realistic Thought |
> |---|---|---|---|---|---|
> | 1. Ex: friend cancels coffee date. | "She doesn't care about me." | Taking it personally. | 1. She cancelled the last time too. 2. We haven't spent much time together lately. | 1. She's been calling and trying to get together. 2. She's been really busy at work. 3. She's been a committed friend for five years. | "She's busy and over-whelmed." |

We encourage you to practice this skill of identifying and challenging your negative thoughts. You can create a blank copy of the
table above in your journal, and fill it out whenever something happens that you find upsetting. Learning to identify thinking errors
takes time and practice, so try to fill out one of these tables completely each day for a week, to get the hang of it. Then, when you

notice your mood has suddenly plummeted, you'll be able to use this skill on the spot and turn that sour mood around!

Increase Positive Feelings through Activity Scheduling

Besides trying to counter your negative thinking, the other major technique in breaking the depression cycle is getting active and engaged in your life again. But this can be very challenging. If you are depressed, you often feel like behaving in a manner that sinks you deeper into depression. You have no energy to get things done around the house, so it becomes messy and disorganized, which makes you feel worse. You may say to yourself, "I am just too tired to exercise," or "I don't feel like eating," so you stop taking care of yourself physically. If you are unproductive at work because of fatigue and difficulty concentrating, you start calling in sick, falling even further behind. Because you don't have the energy to see others or you feel you won't be good company, you withdraw from friends and family, and find yourself isolated.

Simply put, if you give in to your depression, you'll get more depressed. But if you want to become less depressed, you have to overcome your strong desire to withdraw from others and life. This means doing things that you may not want to do at first, such as having lunch with a friend, playing basketball, going for a walk—but if you can muster enough energy to do them, you will start feeling much better.

Research has shown that one of the most effective ways to combat depression is to get active and engage in fun, pleasurable, and social activities. Your brain needs this kind of positive stimulation when it is depressed. Scheduling positive activities is a behavioral

102   Conquering Post-Traumatic Stress Disorder

therapy technique that has been shown to improve depression as much as antidepressant medication. The hard part, as we've just discussed above, is that you don't have the energy or motivation to do much when you are depressed. It is also common to lose a sense of pleasure in the activities you once enjoyed, from reading to hobbies to going out with friends. Over time you stop doing the things you once loved, and as you have fewer positive experiences, you start to feel even worse. People who are depressed also withdraw from relationships, because they feel their negative moods and attitudes will put others off. The problem is, social contact and support are absolutely essential for people who are depressed (and for people who have PTSD!).

Skill 3 for combating depression requires you to do something that will be difficult in the beginning: You need to set aside time to be with others and to do activities you found enjoyable before you were depressed. There is deep wisdom in the slogan, "Fake it until you make it," offered by many 12-step recovery programs. By engaging in pleasurable activities, you will jump-start that part of your brain that experiences positive feelings. Even if you get just five minutes of pleasure from spending several hours with your friends, that's a great start. If you can force yourself to schedule some activities, your mind and brain will slowly remember what it feels like to laugh, have fun, be silly, find interest, and feel involved. Over time, you'll find you want to do these activities, and your depression will start to lift.

Do any of these pleasurable activities appeal to you?

Walking, jogging	Helping someone out
Listening to music	Talking on the phone with a friend
Playing sports	Being in nature, beautiful scenery
Taking a nap	Take a day trip somewhere relaxing

Dinner with friends	Playing with pets
Learning something new	Watching or talking about sports
Working on your car or bike	Calling an old friend
Gardening, landscaping	Getting hair or nails done
Knitting, embroidery, crafts	Playing cards, games
Celebrating a birth, wedding, birthday	Dancing
Spiritual activities, attending services	Going to the movies
Home improvement projects	Doing a hobby
Playing with kids	Shopping
Reading a book, newspaper, magazine	Cooking a good meal
Coffee with friends	Sexual activity
Riding a bike	Camping, hiking, fishing
Building and sitting by a fire	Carpentry
Going to the gym	Hearing a talk, lecture, sermon
Journal writing	Having an open conversation
Singing	Going to a museum or exhibit
Going to the beach or mountains	Performing
Driving for pleasure	Relaxing alone
Throwing a party or attending one	Eating out
Doing artwork	Spending time with family
Taking a bath	Playing music
Doing a good deed	Seeing live music or a show

Step 1: Make a List

Use these examples to identify some activities you enjoy, then make your own list of "Activities I Used to Find Enjoyable and Engaging" organized into "solo" and "social" activities, in your journal. Remember that even if you don't feel like doing the activities now, focus on things that you found fun, fulfilling, engaging, or pleasurable before you were depressed or developed PTSD. Include activities that you might do on your own, such as working on a hobby or going for a walk, and activities that involve other people, perhaps going to lunch with a friend, playing a sport, or enrolling in a class.

Step 2: Make a Commitment

You've got your list. Now, get a calendar and write down what you are willing to commit to in your journal. You will want to schedule several activities each week, and follow through with them—overcoming the blues requires a commitment. Start slow, perhaps scheduling one solo activity and one social activity per week for a month. The solo activity might involve spending half an hour cooking your favorite dessert, working on your car, or reading a book in the sun. The social activity could be scheduling a lunch or going to a movie with a friend. In the beginning, it will be difficult and maybe not much fun, but you'll quickly discover that it becomes easier with time and practice. Also, you may want to ask a friend to help you get going, someone who will either do things with you or check in to make sure you are following your schedule.

If you engage in the pleasurable activities you once enjoyed, you'll rediscover that there is life beyond your trauma. By forcing yourself to enjoy your old hobby even for a few minutes, you will reawaken part of yourself. These enjoyable feelings, however small, should be cultivated like a garden gone fallow. Don't fall into the depression spiral by thinking, "I'll start doing fun things when I feel better." It actually works the other way around: You will start feeling better after you begin doing fun things.

We can't emphasize enough the importance of scheduling activities with other people. Our brains hunger for and thrive on social connection; just being around others is essential to our well-being. Research has shown that people who have broad-based social support systems live longer, recover from illnesses quicker, and get sick less often than people with few social contacts. People who are lonely and isolated suffer more from mental illness, particularly depression. Our social interactions help us feel wanted, appreciated, and accepted; loneliness is associated with higher levels of depression, depleted immune systems, and a much higher risk for suicide. Instead of cutting yourself off from people, you need to take advantage of what social contacts you do have.

Consider this interaction with others to be medicine for your social brain, which we'll talk more about in chapter 8. It is perfectly fine to fake it in the beginning—you don't have to expect to get a lift from your initial contacts. In the long run, though, you will feel much better after spending time with others. By simply increasing your contact with people you help pull yourself out of depression and begin healing.

What commitments will you make this week? Write them in your journal.

1. (solo)_____

2. (social)_____

Skill 4

Exercise as a Powerful Depression Treatment

There is a film shown in high school physical education classes that features a man who is so depressed that he wants to kill himself. The man decides that the best way to do this is to run as long and as far as he can, to induce a heart attack. One day he tries to run beyond exhaustion; he doesn't die. The next day he tries again, running even farther; still, he doesn't die. Every day, he runs farther than the day before, but he does not die. Soon, he finds that he begins to feel different. He's no longer suicidal. In fact, his depression begins to lift! The man decides to keep on running—not to kill himself, but to keep from killing himself.

While everyone knows that exercise is good for your body, not everyone knows that exercise is also a powerful treatment for depression. Many scientific studies have shown that exercise can reduce depressive symptoms. Exercise also produces a tranquilizing effect on the nervous system: The biochemical changes that occur as a result of physical exertion dampen anxiety.

The problem is, like scheduling and following through on enjoyable activities, exercise requires energy and motivation, both of which are in short supply when you are depressed. It's not uncommon for people who had exercised on a regular basis to stop when they experience depression. It's an even bigger hurdle for those who didn't exercise before their depression. But even a small amount of exercise—for instance, walking 30 minutes a day, three days a week—can make a big difference.

What excuses have you used to avoid exercising? Look at the list below, and then at the reasons why the excuses aren't really valid.

Reason	Contradiction
• I'm just too tired to exercise.	• Exercise will actually increase your energy level over time.
• I don't have the time.	• But you may have enough time to watch television. Everyone has time, and it is just a matter of what you choose to do with it.
• I don't belong to any gyms.	• Most forms of exercise can be done outside of a health club.
• I'm not athletic.	• Walking or running requires no athletic ability.
• I can't walk in my neighborhood.	• Most people have cars or access to buses. You can easily drive or take a bus to a park.

Now consider the many positive effects of exercise on your physiology, which improves your depression by altering your brain chemistry.

- Exercise enhances the amount of oxygen in your blood. When your blood is transported to your brain, you feel alert and calm.

- Exercise lowers the acidity (pH) in your body, which increases your energy level.

- Exercise increases seratonin and norepinephrine in the brain—the very same chemicals that are boosted by anti-depressant medications.

- Finally, many people have talked about a runner's high. This feeling of well-being results from the release of our body's endorphins, which are natural brain opiates. Not only do you experience a euphoric and mellow feeling after you exercise, your stress hormones are reduced.

There are many ways to exercise. Some methods require planning; others you can do on the spur of the moment. Getting stress-reducing exercise does not mean going to an expensive health club, suiting up in expensive workout gear, or running five miles a day. Walking is the easiest, cheapest, and most natural form of exercise available to you. You can walk around your neighborhood, in a park, or on a treadmill.

Research has specifically shown that walking is an antidepressant. In one study, researchers divided a group of depressed people into two groups of walkers and non-walkers. They also made sure that neither group received any type of treatment for depression. At the end of the study, the researchers found that the group of walkers became less depressed.

Exercise

Any kind of exercise counts. Even strenuous yard work and house cleaning can give you an aerobic boost. Here are some additional ideas—some of these may be on your pleasurable activities list!

Options for Exercise

Walking around neighborhood	Scrubbing the floor
Playing basketball	Raking the leaves
Climbing stairs	Walking to work or to the store
Going to the gym	Biking
Hiking	Playing soccer or baseball
Shoveling snow	Jogging, running
Walking the dog	Lifting weights
Vacuuming the house	Swimming, surfing
Dancing (at a club or at home)	Running around with kids
Bowling	Gardening

Again, exercise requires a commitment. Look at the pleasurable activities you scheduled this week. If your solo and social activities do not involve exercise, add some form of exercise, for 30 minutes, two or three times this week.

Skill 5

Letting in the Light

Many people have told us that they keep the draperies drawn at home because they "do not want to let the outside world in." Apparently they don't know that low levels of light have been associated with depression. It's more than the idea that opening the draperies means opening yourself to the outside world. It's a biochemical fact.

Your brain picks up signals from your retina about whether it is dark or light outside. If it's dark, your pineal gland secretes a hormone called melatonin to sedate you and allow you to go to sleep. Melatonin is nature's sedative, a hormone that is very similar in chemical structure to serotonin. When there is an overabundance of melatonin in your system, it competes with serotonin, sending down serotonin levels in your body. And low serotonin is connected to depression.

This mechanism is at work in the cases of people who suffer from seasonal affective disorder (SAD). People with SAD often find themselves becoming more depressed during the seasons when there are fewer hours of daylight. A disproportionate number of people in the northwestern United States and northern Europe suffer from SAD because of the overcast skies and short winter days. We are amazed by the number of times people have told us that they only realized how depressed they had been after they gained more daily exposure to sunlight and started to feel better.

Letting in the Light

How can you let more light into your life, especially in the winter months? A few simple things can make a big difference:

- Keep draperies open so that in the morning, the natural sunlight will help your body get on a regular circadian rhythm.

- Try to maximize your exposure to natural sunlight by spending even a small amount of time outside during the day. Take your lunch break outdoors (even if it's cold!), go on a brief walk, or exercise outside.

- Look into a light-therapy device that mimics natural light. You can sit in front of these lights while you read or work; some are designed to increase in brightness gradually in the early morning, to simulate dawn's light.

Moving Forward

While all of these skills are important for improving your mood, you must also take care of your body. We've already talked about how exercise can reduce depression, but you also need to pay attention to what you eat and how you sleep, and be careful about the amount of alcohol or other medications you put in your body.

Your physical health has a profound effect on your brain, and can make your PTSD and depression either much better or much worse. The next section of this book, Taking Care of Your Brain and Body, is dedicated to these topics.

SECTION 3

Taking Care of Your Brain and Body

CHAPTER 6

Sleeping, Eating, and Medication: Ways to Promote a Healthy Brain

Ian

After the trauma, Ian had trouble going to sleep and staying asleep for more than four hours. He had stopped going to the gym, and at night he would lie awake feeling like his body was pulsating with energy. He started staying up late surfing the Internet, and when he finally got to sleep after an hour in bed, he would wake up in a cold sweat from a nightmare. It was no surprise that Ian was exhausted during the day and had trouble concentrating; sometimes, he left work early to nap at home. What he didn't realize was that his irregular hours, napping—and maybe even staring at his computer late into the evening—were making his insomnia worse. When Ian learned that there were simple behavioral changes he could make to improve his sleep, he was able to regain his energy and focus during the day. He also found that he was less irritable at work.

■

Angela

When Angela was referred to a psychiatrist about two years after Katrina, the psychiatrist diagnosed her with PTSD and depression and prescribed an antidepressant for her. Initially, she was very reluctant to take it. Even though her grief over her mother's death wasn't getting any better and she was suffering with severe anxiety and having trouble working, Angela thought that taking medication would mean she was crazy or weak. But after her sister and doctor persuaded her to try an antidepressant medication, she was surprised to find that her dark mood started to lift in the mornings, and she felt calmer. Together with her therapy work, Angela started to make progress working on her grief, anxiety, and avoidance.

Most people know that it's important to take care of your body to be healthy and reduce the long-term risk of illness. But you may not know that your physical health affects all aspects of your well-being: your energy level, mood, ability to concentrate and stay motivated, your desire to socialize, and whether you easily bounce back from stressful problems at work or home. Have you ever quickly downed a soda on an empty stomach, and 20 minutes later felt not only your energy crash but your motivation and mood too? It has to do with the close relationship among your body, brain, and mind. What you put into your body, how much rest your get, and how well all the various chemicals in your brain are interacting can make a huge difference in your emotional well-being and resilience.

Unfortunately, PTSD often disrupts sleep and appetite, interfering with the healthy functioning of your body and making your symptoms even worse. In order to take care of both your physical and emotional health as you work to combat PTSD, this chapter offers you techniques for improving your sleep and making sure you are eating healthy. Because medication can also be very helpful for some individuals working to overcome a trauma, we'll provide information about the common medications for PTSD and some things to consider before deciding whether to start, stop, or continue. The thing to keep in mind is that you must take care of your body to take care of your brain. Your brain, after all, is an essential player in your recovery from PTSD!

Sleeping Better

Insomnia is a common problem for people with PTSD. You may find that you can't shut your mind off at night, or that you toss and turn for hours before going to sleep. Or you may get to sleep just fine, but wake up in the middle of the night or very early in the morning and have trouble getting back to sleep. Often sleep can feel like a war: You are haunted by nightmares, waking up drenched in sweat and so agitated that you have to get out of bed.

There are many reasons why PTSD leads to insomnia. Stress and anxiety activate hormones that can interfere with your normal 24-hour sleep-wake cycle—your body's circadian rhythm. But also, you may further disrupt your body's natural cycle from daily activities such as drinking too much caffeine, keeping an irregular sleep schedule, drinking alcohol before bed, not exercising, or working on your computer late into the night, among others. You may do things you think will help you get to sleep, when in actuality they interfere with it. In this chapter we will describe things you want to avoid and practices that you want to employ to get your sleep back on track.

How Stress Disrupts Your Sleep

Many people are surprised to learn that sleep is not simply a state of unconscious rest: There are actually stages of sleep in which the brain is doing different things.

When you first drift into sleep, you are in stage 1, a transition state from which you can be easily awakened. As your brain waves start to slow, you move into stage 2 sleep, which is a light sleep. During stage 3 your brain starts to produce very slow delta waves, mixed with faster waves; stage 4 is dominated by delta waves. Stages 3 and 4 are considered deep, restorative sleep. It's very hard to wake someone up during this period and there is little eye movement or muscle activity.

What's interesting is that you don't stay in deep sleep. You drift back into stages 3 and then 2, as if you are waking up, but then you move into a stage in which your brain looks active and awake: Rapid Eye Movement (REM) sleep. REM, which is more like stage 1 than deep sleep, is the dreaming stage. Your eyes move back and forth, your breath becomes shallow, blood pressure rises, and your muscles are paralyzed (which thankfully keeps you from acting out your dreams!). This whole cycle takes about 90 minutes, and then repeats again over and over throughout the night. The REM stage gets longer as the night progresses.

Sleep cycles are carefully regulated by the brain through various hormones, which follow a daily circadian rhythm partly tied to day and night. Your stress hormone cortisol, which also follows a daily rhythm, is supposed to be at its lowest level before sleep. But if you are anxious, it will be elevated at the end of the day, making it hard for you to go to sleep. Stress also interferes with deep, slow-wave sleep (which is why you feel exhausted the next day) and REM sleep.

Depression can also affect your sleep, and can shift the amount of REM sleep people have, making them go into REM earlier in the night and wake up earlier. This suggests the circadian rhythm and all of the associated hormones are disrupted in depression as well. Unfortunately, many of the body's immune activities, memory consolidation, and overall body maintenance follow the sleep-wake cycle: When sleep is disrupted, so are these vital activities of the body.

There are several types of insomnia that are common in PTSD. If you have early insomnia, you have difficulty getting to sleep; like Ian, it may take you hours. If you have sleep maintenance insomnia, you have difficulty staying asleep. You may fall asleep without difficulty, but wake up in the middle of the night and have trouble getting back to sleep. With both types of insomnia, at least an hour goes by while you lay in bed trying to sleep. Keep in mind that you may overestimate the time that it takes for you to get to sleep, and don't worry if you can't get to sleep right away—few people can go to sleep within 15 minutes. Some people with PTSD also have early-waking insomnia—waking up at 4:00 a.m. or 5:00 a.m.—though this is more common with depression.

Nightmares are also a common symptom of PTSD, as memories of the trauma pop into your consciousness without your being able to control them. Getting more consistent, quality sleep can sometimes reduce the frequency or intensity of nightmares. Researchers have also found that working through the trauma memory (see chapters 11 and 12), while temporarily increasing intrusive memories and thoughts, reduces nightmares in the longer term. In addition, there are some medications that can help with nightmares, described in the section below.

Now that you have mastered the mini-course on sleep, you are ready to get a good night's rest! There are a number of things you can do to improve the quality of your sleep—and we say quality, because it's more than a matter of the number of hours you sleep or if you wake up in the middle of the night. You want to get your body into a rhythm where it naturally gets the right amount of sleep in the different stages. Because many substances can disrupt REM and deep sleep, sleep killers need to be avoided. Instead, adopt sleep promoters, such as setting and keeping a schedule so that you can get your body's sleep hormones into a predictable circadian rhythm.

SKILL 1

For Better Zzzzzs: Avoid the Sleep Killers

Many people try to get more sleep by using techniques that actually exacerbate their sleep problem. For people with PTSD, these usually include drinking alcohol before going to bed or taking over-the-counter sleep aids. Other activities that can interfere with sleep include consuming caffeine late in the day, smoking or chewing tobacco, keeping your bedroom too warm at night, and using the computer late into the night.

Drinking alcohol at night is probably the biggest sleep-deterrent. Though you may feel sedated and ready to sleep after drinking a nightcap, alcohol can create a sleep problem, even if you don't have PTSD. Alcohol contributes to reducing the deepest stage of sleep (stage 4) and REM sleep. As it wears off, it can also wake you up in the middle of the night, known as mid-sleep-cycle awakening. Once you move into deeper sleep, alcohol disrupts the quality of sleep's important stages, so that in the morning, although you think you've slept, you feel exhausted and groggy. To avoid the problem, do not drink heavily in the evening (no more than two drinks for men, one for women), and do not drink any alcohol several hours before bedtime.

Far too many people also resort to using over-the-counter sleep aids, commonly called sleeping pills. If you've used sleeping pills, you've probably found that although you go to sleep, the quality of your sleep is poor and you end up feeling less rested in the morning. Like alcohol, many sleeping pills suppress important stages of sleep, and they can also lead to tolerance and withdrawal— in other words, you will need more of the drug to achieve the same effect. Later, when you try to sleep without the medication, you will have a more difficult time sleeping than if you had never used it. If you are taking prescribed sleeping pills, talk to your doctor about using them sparingly. If you are using over-the-counter sleeping pills, don't stop them abruptly: Slowly reduce your dose and try to phase them out over time. And if you are not using them now, don't start!

Caffeine is a problem too. Found in coffee, tea, hot chocolate, sodas, and energy drinks, caffeine acts as a stimulant. It specifically blocks a chemical in the brain that promotes sleep, including slow-wave sleep. Tobacco products such as cigarettes and chewing tobacco are also stimulants and can interfere in your ability to wind down and go to sleep. Eating a large meal or snack high in carbohydrates right before bed can interfere with sleep by boosting your levels of sugar, insulin, and the stress hormone cortisol, right when these levels should be at their lowest.

Napping can interfere with sleep, too, particularly if the nap is an hour or longer. If you get tired during the day, try doing something relaxing such as reading a magazine, but resist the urge to lie down and nap. Some people can power nap for 10 or 15 minutes and wake up feeling refreshed, which probably isn't a problem for getting to sleep later. In general, though, try to stay active during the day, so you are tired and ready for bed by night. Also avoid using your computer in the late evening, because the bright computer screen tricks your brain into thinking it's still daytime and suppresses the secretion of melatonin, a chemical that makes you sleepy. You need soft light a few hours before going to sleep, to help the melatonin kick in.

Since your brain is geared to pay attention to novelty, you should ensure that there are few sounds to interfere with your falling asleep. Don't keep the television on at night because it will periodically grab your attention and wake you up; in fact, get the TV out of your bedroom. White noise, on the other hand, is boring and monotonous and screens sudden, intrusive noises, such as barking dogs or passing cars. Some people keep a fan on all night long to provide white noise. Another useful technique is use good quality earplugs to filter out noises.

Skill 1 Practice

Avoid the Sleep Killers

- Avoid taking long naps (more than 15 minutes).

- Do not drink more than one or two alcoholic drinks at night or within two hours of sleeping.

- Avoid over-the-counter sleeping aids; if you are currently taking them, slowly reduce the dose over time so you can stop.

- Avoid caffeinated drinks in the afternoon and evening.

- Don't eat a large meal or snacks high in carbohydrates or sugar before going to bed.

- Don't use your computer late into the night or fall asleep to the television.

For Better Zzzzzs: Use Sleep Promoters

Now that you know what to avoid, here are some positive things you can do to improve the quality and length of your sleep. As we described above, your body's awake-sleep cycle is governed by hormones that follow a daily rhythm. When these hormones (such as cortisol and melatonin) are in sync, they will naturally guide your brain and body to follow a predictable pattern of waking up, getting active, slowing down, and sleeping. But when you vary your schedule by going to bed very late, getting up very early, or getting eight hours of sleep one night and four hours the next, these hormones are disrupted, as they are if you take long naps. Such disruptions make it difficult for your brain to manage sleep cycles.

One of the most important things you can do to promote good sleep therefore is to keep a regular schedule. You may need to get your partner to help with this. Decide when you are going to go to bed every night (within about an hour), then develop a ritual to start winding down and relaxing before going to sleep—this is much easier if you haven't napped earlier in the day. The relaxation techniques discussed in chapter 3 can help you calm your mind and muscles. Make sure that the time you spend in bed is only for sleep, bedtime reading, or sex, and don't use your bedroom as an office or place to watch television—those associations will conflict with soothing your mind so you can fall asleep. Then wake up at the same time every day, no matter whether it is a work or school day or the weekend.

If you do nothing else, keeping a regular sleep schedule will make a big difference in how well you sleep, but there are other things that can help, too.

Aerobic exercise not only has a calming, antidepressant effect but also helps you sleep better that night. Exercising during the day pushes your heart rate and body temperature up, but allows enough time for them to drop before you go to bed at night. It also helps to expend nervous energy and tire out your body, so you feel more relaxed when it's time to sleep.

The amount of light you are exposed to during the daytime also affects your sleep. Maximizing your bright light exposure during the day sets your body clock to match the natural day/night cycle of the world around you. Keep your bedroom cool at night, since cool rooms promote the deepest sleep. But it's still okay to take a bath before bed: Hot baths have been found to be helpful as a wind-down activity. Even though your body temperature rises initially, it will drop sharply by the time you are ready to sleep.

Skill 2 Practice

Use Sleep Promoters

- Exercise during the day.

- Expose yourself to natural light during the day.

- Give yourself time to wind down and relax before going to bed.

- Use your bed only for sleeping, bedtime reading, or sex.

- Keep your bedroom dark and cool at night.

- Go to bed at the same time (within an hour) every night.

- Wake up at the same time (within an hour) every day.

Final Word on Sleep: Don't Worry, Don't Force

If you have trouble falling asleep or wake up in the middle of the night and can't go back to sleep, don't worry that you *must* get to sleep. Remember that you can get less than your normal amount of sleep and be fine. It's also fairly common for people to wake up during one of the lighter phases of sleep, and you can be awake for an hour in the middle of the night and still get back into your rhythm again. If you try too hard to go to sleep, your body will release stress hormones that will increase muscle tension, heart rate, and blood pressure. Instead, take it easy and read until you get sleepy. If you toss and turn for more than an hour, get up and go to another room—getting out of bed will allow your body temperature to drop. The next night, your brain will work to make up the lost sleep.

Eating Better

PTSD Can Change Eating Patterns

People with PTSD often show changes in appetite and weight. You may have lost your interest in eating, or feel like eating well is an unfair luxury. Some people with PTSD find the opposite: Stress makes them want to eat more comfort foods. Physiological activation of your alarm system throughout the day can alter appetite and change how you eat.

Ian not only had sleep problems, he also found that he lost all interest in food. He ate erratically throughout the day, often skipping meals and just eating snacks. His weight dropped over the six months after he was assaulted. Nicole found that she tended to overeat as a way to self-soothe. When she felt low, food gave her a positive boost, and it was one of the few activities that did give her pleasure. But it wasn't just any food: It was sweets and snacks that were high in simple carbohydrates. What she didn't realize is that these unhealthy foods were causing her blood-sugar levels to swing up and down—and with them, her mood.

Appetite changes are also a common symptom of depression, a problem for many people with PTSD. More often, depression causes loss of appetite and weight loss, but some people show the opposite pattern. Whether it is anxiety or depression or both that may be affecting your eating, pay attention to what you put in your body—it affects your mind, mood, and well-being.

Food: It Matters What You Put in Your Body

It may be hard to believe that your diet can really affect your PTSD symptoms and emotional states, but it can. You are a biological being, and what you eat has a major effect on your biochemistry and how your brain functions. If you want to maintain balanced moods and clear thoughts, you will need to eat a variety of healthful foods regularly throughout the day. In addition, stress itself has an impact on how your body absorbs and manufacturers nutrients: If you add poor diet to a body already struggling to stay healthy, it's a double-whammy. Since your brain is the highest energy-consumer of all organs in your body, any change in your food intake will have a major impact on its ability to function.

Here's one example of how food affects the brain. Consider the importance of eating protein, which is found in all types of food including meat, milk, and beans. Protein is broken down in the body into amino acids, which serve as crucial building blocks for the brain chemicals called neurotransmitters. These neurotransmitters play a major roll in the way your brain operates; they are the chemicals that your neurons use to communicate with each other, and they affect your thinking and mood.

For example, L-Glutamine is an amino acid found in foods such as almonds and peaches. When L-Glutamine is digested, your body uses it to synthesize into the neurotransmitter called GABA. Each neurotransmitter has specific function in your brain. For example:

Amino Acid	Neurotransmitter	Effects
L-Trytophan	Serotonin	Improves sleep calmness and mood
L-Glutamine	GABA	Decreases tension and irritability
L-Phenylalanine	Dopamine	Increases feelings of pleasure
L-Phenylalanine	Norepinephrine	Increases energy, feelings of pleasure, and memory

You will be happy to know that you do not need to memorize the names of these amino acids and how they affect your energy moods! The point is simply that what you eat has an impact on your brain and how it functions, and on the health of your body and mind. You do not need to be a biochemist to follow a healthful diet. Several simple principles of eating will ensure that you are getting the nutrition you need to keep your body and brain healthy.

SKILL 3

Eat in a Healthful, Balanced Way to Feel Good

While there are many diets out there all claiming to be the healthiest, there are some basic strategies to eating that almost all scientists will agree upon. Fortunately, they are also common sense. If you have PTSD, it's especially important to follow these simple rules, which center on variety, balance, and whole foods.

Seek out Variety in Your Diet

You should eat a variety of foods. Why? Because your body needs many types of chemicals to function well—including vitamins, minerals, fiber, amino acids, flavinoids, and fatty acids, among others. If you eat the same cereal for breakfast, sandwich for lunch, and take-out burger for dinner every day, you are getting only some of what you need. But if you eat different things every day, you cover your bases and never consume too much of one thing. Vary the fruit you put on your cereal each day; try out some new recipes; add a carrot, celery, or apple to your lunch; order something different at your favorite taco stand.

Balance Your Protein, Carbs, and Fat

Your body needs carbohydrates, proteins, and fats to function. If you've been following any of the recent diet crazes, you may think that one category is bad, while another is good. The key is to balance these basic components of your diet by eating moderate amounts of a variety of foods.

Carbohydrates are basically chains of sugar that are most concentrated in grains (rice, wheat); fruit; legumes (beans and peas); roots (potatoes, carrots); and anything high in starch, flour, or sugar (honey, bread, candy bars). Complex carbs are found in whole grains, fruits, and legumes, and are high in fiber and other nutrients. Simple carbs, like foods made from white flour or with added sugar such as desserts, white bread, or French fries, often lack fiber and other nutritional elements. Carbohydrates are your energy source. But too many carbohydrates—especially simple carbs—can cause energy swings and mood swings, and potentially Type II diabetes. If you've ever reached for that soda or candy bar in the afternoon for an energy boost, you have no doubt experienced the crash soon afterwards.

Protein is primarily found in meat, dairy products, and legumes (beans), and is broken down into amino acids which are essential to making enzymes in the body (such as the neurotransmitters described above). Enzymes carry out all of the body's cell activities. Some amino acids can be produced by the body, but others must be consumed in food. Consuming too much protein, however, can put strain on your kidneys.

Fat is found in animal products (meat, dairy), seeds and nuts, and in vegetable oils. Fat gets broken down into fatty acids, which are also necessary components of many types of enzymes in the body. There has been a lot of attention on the types of fat in food: Saturated fat in meat and dairy should be limited more than mono- and polyunsaturated fats found in vegetable oil. A gram of fat has more than twice the calories as a gram of protein or carbs, which is why too much fat can cause weight gain. High-fat diets are also associated with cardiovascular problems. The key is to eat a moderate amount of the mono- and polyunsaturated fats in your diet.

Eat Whole Foods Not Processed Foods

One of the best ways to get a varied and balanced diet is to eat whole foods such as vegetables, fruits, whole grains (brown rice, oatmeal, sprouted grains, foods made with whole wheat), eggs, fish, meat, and dairy products that are low in saturated fat. These foods contain many nutrients that are essential to your health—and which are often taken out as foods are refined or processed. Refined grains or flour have parts of the plant (the bran or germ) stripped away, as in products such as white sugar, white flour, and white rice. "Processed" usually means that the food item includes refined flour or sugar and many other ingredients and chemicals to improve taste or longevity, but not usually health. Common examples are fries, chips, desserts, most fast food, and bread and pasta made from refined flour.

You may think that you can eat a TV dinner or burger on the run, and make up for your fast-food moment by popping a multivitamin. But research suggests that you should get your nutrients from food, not a pill. The reason is that we don't really understand all of the chemicals that are in food; many are likely to be important, but just haven't been studied. Fruits and vegetables are among the most important sources of nutrients, so follow your grandmother's advice and eat your broccoli!

Graze Your Way through the Day

Research also suggests that eating small meals or snacks throughout the day rather than two or three big meals is better for you. Small meals tend to be easier to digest, and also keep your blood sugar level more even during the day, so you don't have those energy highs and lows. This will help keep your mood more stable as well.

Minimize Caffeine

Think of coffee and other caffeinated drinks as liquid anxiety. Caffeine is a stimulant and increases stress hormones in your body, particularly adrenalin. Large amounts of caffeine put your body into a prolonged state of stress and hyperalertness. In fact, if you consume more than two or three cups of brewed coffee or soft drinks with caffeine, you may experience a wide range of problems, including nervousness, flushed face, muscle twitching, rapid heartbeat, diarrhea, insomnia, restlessness, panic attacks, ringing in the ears, and trembling. And, just like eating sugar and simple carbs, after the caffeine wears off, you usually crash. The caffeine "come down" can result in headaches, fatigue, and difficulty concentrating. Finally, caffeine interferes with sleep, so avoid it in the afternoon or evening.

Skill 3 Practice

Eat in a Healthful, Balanced Way to Feel Good

- Seek out variety in your diet to make sure you are getting all your nutrients.

- Don't eat too much protein, carbs, or fat; keep these in balance to maintain your energy, mood, and health.

- Eat whole foods (rather than processed or refined foods) such as whole grains, legumes, fruits, vegetables, bread made from whole-wheat flour, eggs, fish, meat and dairy low in saturated fat (turkey, chicken, low-fat milk, and yogurt).

- Graze throughout the day instead of eating two or three big meals.

- Keep the amount of caffeine you drink to less than two cups of coffee, tea, or soda.

Take Smart Advantage of Medications

Like Angela, you may have talked to your doctor about medication, but have some reservations about taking it. You may feel it's embarrassing, or may not fully understand what you were prescribed or why. We'll describe below some of the more common types of medications prescribed for symptoms of PTSD. Many of these—such as antidepressants, sleep medications, and mood stabilizers—can be extremely helpful in the treatment of trauma. Some, such as the group of medications known as benzodiazepines, you'll want to be cautious about. Being informed and cautious is key.

Why You Might Not Want to Take Medications

Many people feel there is a stigma associated with medications for a mental health problem. Even though you may understand that conditions like depression and PTSD clearly involve both psychological and physical components, you may resist your doctor's suggestion to try a medication, or to stay on it. While you probably wouldn't object to medication for high cholesterol or allergies, you may feel that taking medication for PTSD or depression means that you are mentally or morally weak.

But you might try thinking about it differently. Your brain is still part of your body, and there are symptoms that you cannot control by sheer force of will. You should treat anxiety or depression just as seriously and aggressively as you would a heart condition. And, as with heart disease, there are medications you can take and behavioral changes you can make that will help. We encourage you to think carefully about all the pros and cons of taking medication, and not let shame or stigma keep you from taking something that might really bring you some relief. If your doctor has prescribed medication such as an antidepressant for your PTSD, consider taking it, and also work through the exercises in this book. Together, they can help to improve your physical and mental health.

While there is no single medication type that is specific for PTSD, the following is a brief description of some of the more common medications prescribed to treat some of the symptoms. Research suggests that antidepressants are often helpful for PTSD, and sleep medications may be necessary if you've unsuccessfully tried the behavioral suggestions above. Benzodiazepine medications such as Xanax are frequently prescribed to reduce anxiety quickly, but this class of medication can be habit-forming and may interfere with behavioral efforts to reduce anxiety over time. Finally, there are some additional classes of medications, such as mood stabilizers and antipsychotic medications, that are sometimes prescribed for PTSD. Read on to learn more, and also ask your doctor any questions you may have about medications.

Antidepressants Can Often Be Helpful

Antidepressant medications are prescribed for both depression and anxiety. Many people with PTSD can benefit from antidepressants: They can help with sleep problems, appetite changes, sadness or distress, panic attacks, and fatigue. Some can also help with unwanted intrusive memories of trauma. Antidepressants do not make you suddenly feel better, which is why they are not addictive or sold on the street as recreational drugs. They act slowly, and it may take anywhere from two to four weeks before you'll notice any benefits. Most people take antidepressants for at least six months and often for years, and research shows that they tend to be relatively safe for adults.

Most antidepressants fall into one of three broad classes: the tricyclic antidepressants, the MAO inhibitors, and the newer selective seratonin reuptake inhibitors (SSRIs). The tricyclic antidepressants, such as Tofranil (imipramine), Elavil (amitriptyline), and the newer tetracyclic antidepressant Remeron (mirtazapine), tend to work on two important neurotransmitters related to depression and anxiety: serotonin and norepinephrine. They are effective in treating both depression and anxiety, but they can cause "anti-cholinergic" side effects including dry mouth, constipation, difficulty urinating, and blurry vision. It's very important not to drink alcohol when taking a tricyclic antidepressant. The MAOs, such as Nardil (phenelzine), work on serotonin, norepinephrine, and dopamine and are also effective. They have strict dietary restrictions, however, including red wines; beers; smoked, aged, or pickled meat or fish; and aged cheeses. If you eat any of these foods while taking an MAO inhibitor, you can have a dangerous and sometime lethal rise in blood pressure.

The SSRIs, such as Prozac (fluoxetine), Paxil (paroxetine), Zoloft (sertraline), and Celexa (citalopram), are the mostly commonly prescribed class of antidepressants for depression and anxiety disorders such as PTSD, panic disorder, social anxiety, and obsessive-compulsive disorder. Studies comparing the SSRIs to placebos have demonstrated that SSRIs are effective in reducing many of the symptoms of PTSD, including intrusive memories, emotional numbing, and avoidance. Like all antidepressants, SSRIs have a variety of side effects including nausea, nervousness, dry mouth, loose bowel movements, sedation, and sexual dysfunction (drop in interest, arousal, and erectile problems). In general, SSRIs tend to have fewer side effects and are less dangerous than the tricyclics or MAOs, which is why doctors typically prefer them. The other two classes of medications, however, have less frequent sexual side effects.

Some physicians fail to warn patients that the medications have side effects that can be intense in the beginning, but often fade in time. This is why dosages of most antidepressant medications are slowly increased during the first weeks, giving your body time to adjust to the medication. But if you are unaware of potential side effects in the beginning, you may suddenly stop taking them. Work with your doctor to make sure you stay on your medication long enough to see if the side effects diminish and whether the medication is effective. You may have to try several different antidepressants before you find the best one for you.

Limit Your Use of Benzodiazapine Medications

If you complain to your doctor that you are stressed out or have anxiety, he or she may give you a medication such as Xanax or Ativan, which are benzodiazapine medications that are indeed effective at reducing anxiety. That's why they are prescribed more than any other type of medication: When a patient comes into a physician's office feeling distressed, the doctor often will choose to prescribe something that will have an immediate effect. Unfortunately, the quick relief may not be sustained and may require an increase in dose to maintain a beneficial effect. As a result, the benzodiazepines can be habit-forming.

The benzodiazapines ("benzos" for short) include Valium (diazepam), Ativan (lorazepam), and Xanax (alprazolam). These drugs act on the neuotransmitter GABA, which has a calming effect on the brain. They are referred to as minor tranquilizers, or anti-anxiety agents, and are sometimes prescribed for problems with sleep. When used occasionally, they are not problematic. But because benzos quickly reduce anxiety, much like a shot of whiskey or glass of wine would, people tend to start using them regularly and can become dependent on them. And just like alcohol or any other quick fix, benzos tend to perpetuate anxiety in the long term. If you pop a Xanax whenever you get anxious, your brain never learns that the situation is not dangerous and that you will be fine without your drug. Instead, taking a pill when you're anxious reinforces the sense of danger and your dependency on the medication. Benzos can be difficult to quit if you've been taking them regularly—the withdrawal effects can be significant.

In addition to being habit-forming, benzos have a number of negative side effects. They can make some people feel depressed, and they also have a tendency to cloud your thinking and dampen your short-term memory. These issues are troubling, because your clarity of thought and memory are crucial for developing the coping strategies taught in this book.

If you are taking benzos regularly, we recommend you work with your doctor to slowly start reducing the dose and frequency. It will take time and patience, but set a goal to be benzo-free after a month or two. If you have a prescription but don't use benzos regularly, keep it that way! And if you don't have a prescription and a doctor offers you one, consider saying no. Your recovery from PTSD will be easier without them.

Be Cautious with Sleep Medications

As mentioned above, sleep problems are one of the most common symptoms of PTSD. Before you turn to medication to improve your sleep, we recommend that you first try to make the behavior changes described in skills 2 and 3 above. These "sleep hygiene" skills are widely recommended by mental health professionals, and can really make a difference. But if you still have sleep problems that make it difficult for you to function during the day, even after you've made these behavior changes, talk to your doctor about a medication to help with sleep. There are a number of different medications that can be helpful; always avoid over-the-counter sleep aids.

Other Medications for PTSD

Sometimes doctors prescribe other types of medication for PTSD, including mood stabilizers, atypical antipsychotic medications, and hypertensive medications. As with any other drug, be sure to understand the nature, risks, and benefits of trying these medications, especially because these are less researched for PTSD.

The mood stabilizers, including Depakote (valproate), Lamictal (lamotrigine), Topamax (topiramate), Tegretol (carbamazepine), and lithium are regularly prescribed for bipolar disorder (manic depression), but they can also help people with PTSD reduce intense mood symptoms and intrusive memories of the trauma. The atypical antipsychotic medications such as Zyprexa (olanzapine) and Risperdal (risperidone) are prescribed for problems such as feeling "amped up" and hypervigilant, or for reducing aggressive behavior, nightmares, and intrusive thoughts and images. They have a tranquilizing effect, so they can make people feel tired. These two classes of medication have a variety of potential side effects. You need to carefully discuss their benefits and risks with your doctor before taking them.

Finally, medications to treat hypertension are occasionally prescribed to treat PTSD symptoms. Minipress (prazosin) has been found to be helpful for relieving the frequency and intensity of nightmares. Inderal (propranolol) may be helpful for PTSD arousal and re-experiencing symptoms.

SKILL 4

Take Smart Advantage of Medications

- If your doctor recommends a medication for your PTSD, be open to the possibility that it may be helpful. Think honestly about the pros and cons, and don't let stigmas get in the way of your recovery.

- Always understand what you are taking, the side effects and risks, and when you should expect to see some improvement in your symptoms.

- Antidepressants can reduce the anxiety and depression associated with PTSD. If your doctor has recommended it, be sure to take the medication long enough to see the side effects decrease and any benefits take effect (two to four weeks).

- Limit your benzo use (such as Xanax and Ativan). These medications are habit-forming; the short-term relief they bring is often at the cost of longer-term improvement.

- Be cautious about prescribed sleep medication (certain types can be habit-forming), and resist over-the-counter sleep aids.

- Understand the risks and benefits of any other medication prescribed for PTSD, especially if it has not been widely studied for the disorder.

Moving Forward

Improving your sleep, eating healthy, and taking smart advantage of medications—these are some things you can do to take care of your body and brain, which in turn will help to reduce PTSD symptoms and improve your mood. In chapter 5 we also talked about the importance of exercise, which research clearly shows is an effective antidepressant itself; be sure to integrate it into your daily routine.

In the next chapter, we'll talk about some of the behaviors that can hurt your body and brain, and generally make your PTSD symptoms worse, including excessive alcohol and illicit drug use. Even if you are a moderate drinker or user, we encourage you to read through this chapter and do the exercises. Remember that everything you put into your body, especially substances that directly affect brain function, will impact your PTSD. We want to help you make sure that you are not doing anything to interfere with your recovery from PTSD and your brain's ability to heal.

CHAPTER 7

Reducing Your Dependence on Alcohol and Drugs

Sonya

Sonya noticed that her drinking had increased after the accident. She loved a glass of wine after work to relax, but one glass no longer took care of the anxiety she felt after riding the bus home from work. Soon she was drinking three, occasionally four glasses over the course of the evening. She could tell the drinking was making her less engaged with Eric, her son, which made her feel guilty and depressed. Sometimes she felt hung over the next day. She also knew that she had become dependent on her Xanax prescription for anxiety. She was taking three pills a day to get her through, and couldn't imagine getting on the morning bus without it. But she was tired of using substances to cope. She wanted to get her strength back, be a better mom to Eric, and have more control over her symptoms. Sonya committed to cutting back.

Dan

Dan and his buddies drank regularly in Iraq, and the drinking continued when he got back. It was what he and his friends did when they got together at the sports bar, but he also took to drinking Jack Daniels or smoking marijuana at home whenever the memories of combat would pop up or he felt anxious or angry. He also drank or smoked to try to sleep, and woke up feeling rotten, tired, and irritable. He knew his substance use was driving some of his moods and especially his fights with his wife, Heather. She thought he had a real problem, and had threatened to move out. When his therapist at the VA told him that his drinking and marijuana use were making his PTSD worse and that it would be hard to get better unless he cut back or stopped, he decided he would give it try.

■

Many people with PTSD use alcohol and other substances as a quick way to reduce their stress or blunt negative feelings. You may feel you need your drink or anti-anxiety medication such as Xanax to reduce your anxiety or get to sleep. Maybe you think that you deserve a few indulgences such as alcohol or marijuana because of how hard it is to live with PTSD.

You know these substances bring temporary relief, but you may not know that they can make the symptoms and problems of PTSD worse. In this chapter, we talk about the ways in which many traumatized individuals such as Dan and Sonya turn to alcohol and other drugs to escape their symptoms. While these substances do lower anxiety in the moment, in the long run excessive substance use actually will worsen anxiety, depression, mood swings, and sleep problems. Alcohol also tends to increase anger and relationship conflict, and interferes with functioning at home and work.

If you use substances to self-medicate your anxiety and depression, you may want to consider different ways of coping and relaxing that are empowering and healthful. This chapter will help you explore the reasons for and against your drinking or drug-use behavior, and show you how to cut back or quit, if you are ready to change. The alternatives are geared toward using your strength and resiliency to cope more effectively with PTSD.

Substance Use and PTSD: Some Things You Might Not Know

The reason people have a drink after work, down a few beers with friends, or light up a joint after a stressful day is because it often makes them feel better—temporarily, at least. Of course, this is why there's such a high demand for these substances. Alcohol does have an effect on the brain to help you unwind and relax, and it can also ease social anxiety, relieve boredom, and make activities more "fun." Marijuana has many similar effects. Sounds good, no?

The problem is that there is a big difference between having a glass of wine with dinner and having one or two bottles a night. Most people know that excessive drinking causes significant health problems and can impair memory, thinking, and judgment. But alcohol and drug use also cause changes in the brain, which increase irritability, anxiety, depression, and anger. And contrary to what most people believe, even small amounts of alcohol actually disrupt deep sleep and REM (the dreaming stage), so that you don't get the restorative rest you need.

Let's separate the myths from the realities about alcohol, much of which is also true about marijuana.

Common myths:

- Alcohol is a sleep aid.

- Alcohol lifts one out of depression.

- Alcohol decreases stress.

- Alcohol decreases anxiety.

The reality:

- Alcohol will help you fall asleep, but it disrupts deep (restorative) sleep and REM, so that you feel less rested and alert the next day.

- Alcohol can cause short-term memory problems and impair thinking, productivity, and judgment.

- Alcohol decreases interest and motivation in the long term.

- Alcohol affects neurotransmitters in the brain that increase anxiety, irritability, and depression after use.

When Should You Be Concerned?

Is your substance use problematic? Sometimes it's hard to tell. There is a difference between use (having an occasional drink or two) and abuse (when it starts to have a negative impact on your life). Where you draw the line may also be different for people with PTSD. There are two reasons for this. The first is that there can be a strong pull to drink or use drugs as a way to self-medicate the anxiety symptoms and blunt other negative emotions such as grief, sadness, and shame; individuals who normally don't imbibe often may find themselves drinking or lighting up more often. Second, even small quantities of alcohol or marijuana can increase anxiety and depression symptoms over time, which is usually not an issue for people who do not have PTSD.

If you have experienced a trauma and are struggling with PTSD, we recommend you take a more conservative stand on alcohol or drug use. You can also ask yourself these questions:

1. Do you automatically turn to drugs or alcohol when you feel anxious?

2. Are you using substances to manage your anxiety or moods?

3. Do you need a drink or smoke to go out and do things in the world or be social?

If you said yes to any of these, even if your use is small or infrequent, it may be that you are trying to manage your anxiety with alcohol or drugs. They have become a crutch for your PTSD. Consider using healthful strategies that are more empowering and do not have the negative side effects on your thinking and mood, which we talk about below.

The problems that alcohol and other drug use cause obviously increase with the amount and frequency of use. Heavy substance use will make it very difficult to overcome PTSD, and there are additional negative consequences. Take a few moments to consider the following questions.

1. Do you drink or use every day? Would it be hard not to?

2. Do you frequently consume or use more than you intended?

3. Have you tried to cut back but had difficulty succeeding?

4. Do you find you need to drink or use more to get the same effect?

5. Have you ever had withdrawal symptoms when you stopped?

6. Do friends or family comment or complain about your use?

7. Does your use interfere with your productivity at school or work?

8. Does your use interfere with your family responsibilities or engagement?

9. Is it interfering in any way with your relationships?

10. Do you get into more arguments or fights when you've been drinking or using?

11. Have you ever been arrested for using?

12. Have you ever given up important activities or missed important events because of your use?

13. Do you spend a lot of time, money, or energy using or trying to get alcohol or drugs?

The more questions you answered yes to, the more likely it is that you have moved from use to abuse or dependence.

If you have any concern about your drinking or drug use, you might consider whether you are ready to stop or at least cut back. This is not an easy decision, but we can help. Work through the next sections of this chapter to weigh the pros and cons, and as you do, keep in mind that the costs of using are generally higher for someone with PTSD.

Reasons You May Want to Drink or Use

You may have some concern about your drinking or drug use, but you may also be ambivalent about reducing or giving up your use. This is natural. Part of the process of deciding whether you want to change your drinking habits is to honestly consider the trade-offs. Change requires a commitment, and only you know if you are ready.

We have already talked about some of the reasons people with PTSD like to drink or use drugs. You may use to relax or blunt your anxiety, grief, or other negative emotions. You may use to make socializing or going out easier. You may think it helps with sleep— it doesn't really. Some veterans like to use stimulants like speed to recapture the rush of being in the war zone. If you feel numb, alcohol or drugs can make you feel more alive. You may drink or light up to have fun around others. Or it may feel like using is the only thing that can connect you with others.

Journal Exercise: Your Reasons for Drinking or Using

Write out your list of reasons for drinking or using in your journal.

Reasons You May Want to Cut Back or Stop

Now that you have thought about your reasons for using alcohol or drugs, next consider your reasons for reducing your use or stopping altogether. You can go back to the list of questions above to help you think about this. Consider the impact your drinking or use is having on your relationships, work or school, finances, health, productivity, mood symptoms, and sense of well-being. Remember also that regular or heavy use will interfere with your recovery from PTSD.

Journal Exercise: Your Reasons for Stopping or Cutting Back

Write out your list of reasons for wanting to stop or cut back in your journal.

Are You Ready to Change?

Now that you've listed the pros and cons of drinking or using, it's time to decide whether you are ready to change. You may feel your use is not problematic, and that no change is needed. You may feel somewhat motivated to cut back, or absolutely ready to reduce your use or stop altogether. Only you know if you are ready.

If the answer is no or probably not, we would still encourage you to try to substitute the anxiety management techniques in this book for drinking or using. The next time you are anxious, try doing some slow breathing, or use imagery or progressive muscle relaxation to help you go to sleep. You can also refer to the chapters on depression to help manage your mood, and the chapters on overcoming withdrawal and anger to help increase social activities and connection without needing substances.

If the answer is yes to cutting back, then congratulations on taking a courageous stand for your health and well-being!

Make a Plan to Cut Back or Quit

Your next step is to make a plan, the first part of which is to decide how much you want to cut back. If you are a very heavy user or have struggled for a long time trying to control your drinking or drug use, we recommend abstinence. For some, this is the only way to keep from problematic using. If you feel your using is less problematic, or are simply concerned about how drinking or drug use negatively impacts your PTSD, then you might want to find ways to reduce how often and how much you use.

The second part of your plan is to make a short-term commitment, and test out how it goes. The reason for not making a long commitment is that often it is hard to take that first step toward change. You don't want to set yourself up to feel like a failure if, after one try, you don't change forever. Start with a modest goal to reduce your use for a period of time, and then recommit if the change is working for you.

Journal Exercise: Make a Plan

Write in your journal how much you want to cut back, and make a short-term commitment (one or more months) to follow your plan. You can recommit for a longer period once you meet your first short-term goal.

For example, Dan felt that his drinking and smoking pot were out of control, and he wanted to try abstinence. He made a plan to quit for two months. He talked to Heather about supporting his efforts, he got rid of the alcohol and marijuana in his house, and he started attending Alcoholics Anonymous (AA) meetings. Here's what he had to say about the experience:

> DAN: I knew that the drinking was making my marriage worse, and that if I could just start with a small victory and give up the Jack Daniels and pot for two months, it might clear my head and make reconciliation possible. So I did, and it wasn't as hard as I thought it would be. Heather was great about it. We'd spend time together watching movies at home or going out to eat, and we talked more. I was so sure the drinking was helping my sleep, but when I stopped, I actually felt much less tired and shaky. And what was really amazing is that the roller-coaster moods just mellowed out! I stopped swinging between the highs and lows, stopped lashing out at Heather and guys at work. When we hit the two-month mark, I was ready to commit more seriously and give it up for good.

Sonya also felt that she wanted to cut back on her drinking and Xanax use. She did not have any problem with substance use before her PTSD, and knew that she was using now as a poor way of coping with her symptoms. She made a one-month plan to drink no more than one drink a day, and to taper her Xanax use:

> SONYA: It felt good to make a decision to keep my drinking to one glass of wine with dinner. This was my normal routine before the accident, and I felt pretty confident I could do it. I had been struggling with a lot of shame and guilt for increasing my drinking, especially how out of it I was at night with Eric after three or four drinks. So cutting back the alcohol was easy—I really wanted to do it, and it was no problem doing it for a month. I did this first, and then after I was comfortable with my drinking, I focused on reducing how much Xanax I was taking. This seemed harder and scarier—I wasn't sure I could handle my

anxiety without the Xanax. But I also knew that I wanted to get rid of that crutch, and to some day be able to drive, so I had to be able to manage my anxiety myself to do that. I decided to talk to my doctor and we agreed to cut my dose in half each week: Week one would be two pills a day, then the next week one pill, then a half. The fourth week I would try to have several days during the week in which I wouldn't use Xanax at all. Before I started tapering my Xanax, though, I spent a week really practicing the techniques for riding out anxiety, grounding, and relaxation. And you know, it worked! I still use Xanax sometimes, but I really try to use it only periodically, and never several days in row. And I feel stronger, like I can handle the anxiety when it comes.

Sonya's approach was smart. She didn't try to cut everything out at once, but started with her drinking. When that felt stable, she tackled her Xanax use. She also recognized that cutting back would temporarily increase her anxiety, and that she needed her own tools for managing this. The next section summarizes alternative ways to cope with anxiety and to connect with others.

Substitute Alternative Ways to Cope, Relax, and Enjoy Yourself

Because you use alcohol and drugs for various reasons—to dull negative feelings, to have fun, or to feel comfortable in an anxious situation—you need to develop alternative ways to cope and relax. It is important to feel like you have the power to manage anxiety and other uncomfortable feelings, and to move through your day without the need for any chemical crutches. Many healthful and empowering options have already been introduced in this book, and we encourage you to practice them, as Sonya did, so that you really develop your emotional and behavioral muscles.

You'll want to review these skills:

- To better tolerate anxiety: In chapter 3, review skill 2 (alarm sensations are harmless); skill 3 (riding out anxiety); and skill 4 (grounding techniques).

- To counter anxiety with relaxation: Also in chapter 3, review skill 5 (slow breathing); skill 6 (progressive muscle relaxation); skill 7 (imagery); and skill 8 (prayer and meditation).

- To challenge negative thinking and increase positive feelings: In chapter 5, review skill 2 (challenging negative thinking); skill 3 (scheduling pleasurable activities); and skill 4 (exercise as a mood enhancer).

- To reconnect with others: Review all of the strategies in chapters 8 and 12.

Avoid Situations and Cues that Are Triggers for Substance Use

Along with developing and strengthening your coping skills, it is important to recognize the situations that trigger your drinking or drug use, and either avoid them or develop a plan for handling the situation. Social situations, such as meeting friends at a bar where everyone is drinking, is one typical example. Dan had to decide if he should stop going to the sports bar, or if he would be comfortable just ordering a soda. Sonya needed to anticipate that her anxiety would always go up right before she got on the bus; her plan was to start using the anxiety management techniques a few minutes before and during the bus ride.

Journal Exercise: Triggers and Coping Plan

Write down what situations make you want to drink, smoke marijuana, or use drugs in your journal. Then write down your coping plan for the next time you encounter the situation.

Join a Support Group

If you are like Dan and decide to abstain altogether from drugs and alcohol, there are substance abuse support groups such as Alcoholics Anonymous (AA) that can provide great support. Such groups do tend to require a commitment to abstinence, so if you are just trying to cut back, you may want to look for a group that focuses on PTSD.

Moving Forward

Cutting back or stopping your drinking or drug use is a challenge that requires ongoing effort and repeated tries. The important thing is that you do try, and keep trying, even if you break your commitment to yourself. Keep in mind that most people don't succeed their first time. If you make a short-term commitment and can't stick to it, don't take it as a failure. You just need to think about what went wrong, remind yourself of the reasons you want to stop or cut back, and recommit when you are ready. Remember that changing behavior requires changing habits—it does get easier with practice and time. Every healthy day matters, and every day you succeed in using more empowering techniques to overcome PTSD is a good day. Applaud yourself for your effort and courage!

SECTION 4

Healing Trauma by Improving Relationships

CHAPTER 8

From Withdrawal to Embrace

Barry

Barry was only vaguely aware of how he was pulling away from his family and friends after the fire. His primary way of coping with PTSD was to hole up at home and avoid people as much as possible, even when his wife, Shaundra, and his kids were around. He just couldn't muster the energy to interact with others for long, and he felt self-conscious about his moods and irritability with his family. Barry was also afraid of showing any anxiety in front of his buddies, so he stopped going out with his fellow firefighters after work, and quit his soccer team. Shaundra tried to invite friends over, but Barry objected: He just wanted to be alone.

■

Sonya

Sonya was a shy person by nature, and never had a large social support network. She did not interact much with people at her software company, and knew some of the people at her daughter's school, but not well. Most of her extended family was in New Mexico, and she hadn't tried dating since her divorce four years ago. Because of her intense fear of driving, she became essentially housebound except for going to work. Sonya was isolated. She wished she had someone to talk to, but she felt that her accident and her PTSD had changed her. She feared that others would see her as crazy because of her anxiety symptoms and avoidance.

■

People who have experienced a trauma have a serious dilemma. The nature of PTSD makes most people want to withdraw from others in their lives, yet social relationships are the key to well-being and recovery.

In this chapter, we'll explore how and why you withdraw from others, the importance of social medicine, and how you can make your way back. If you already have family, friends, and existing relationships, we'll offer tools for reconnecting and deepening those connections; if you've not had a large social-support network in the past, we'll show you how to create and nourish new relationships. You'll re-learn how to enjoy spending time with family and friends, to extend yourself to offer and accept invitations, to expand your social circle, and to enrich your life with your partner. It may be difficult at first, but it will be worth it, as you allow the friendship and love of others into your life, to help you heal.

Why People with PTSD Withdraw from Relationships

Withdrawing from friends, coworkers, and family members is one of the most common—and most harmful—responses to trauma. So why do PTSD sufferers do it?

The most obvious reason is the loss of energy and motivation that so often accompany PTSD. If, like Barry and Sonya, you are struggling with anxiety and depression every day, you don't have much energy or positive motivation left over to socialize with others. Just trying to get through work and home responsibilities can make it hard to do anything else.

It is also common for people with PTSD to experience a loss of pleasure in activities they once enjoyed, as we discussed in chapter 5. Like Barry, you may not feel open, engaged, or fun to be around anymore. You might even feel that you've lost some essential part of yourself, leaving you with little to give. This can lead to worry that others won't want to be around you, further reinforcing your desire to withdraw.

The sense that the trauma experience has separated you from others is another reason you might withdraw. You may feel, as Sonya did, that you are different or changed, and that others cannot understand what you have gone through. Trauma is often a life-threatening event that transforms the way you feel about yourself and the world; it's easy to feel estranged from others when they can't truly imagine your experience. You may even feel resentful that other people don't have to struggle with the emotional pain that you have—it feels unfair to be suffering alone. Well-meaning friends and family often don't know how to provide support, and the thought of trying to explain yourself to them may be more than you can put yourself through. You might even wonder if it would be worth it. The result is that you withdraw even more, become more estranged, irritable, and angry, furthering your sense of isolation and alienation.

Another common reason people with PTSD withdraw is embarrassment about the disorder. Both Barry and Sonya feared that others would see their symptoms as signs of weakness, or that there might be something wrong with them. Veterans sometimes worry about the stigma that being labeled "PTSD" by the military places on them. You may also feel shame about the trauma itself; this is especially true with survivors of childhood abuse, but also of adult abuse and rape. Unfortunately, many abuse survivors blame themselves for the trauma and feel they need to hide the truth about what happened to them.

Importance of "Social Medicine" for Recovery

Even though it can be difficult to reach out to others, we cannot emphasize enough how much social support, friendship, and love are essential to your well-being, especially after a trauma. Relationships provide a sense of belonging and of being valued, and are an important source of joy that gives meaning to our lives. People naturally turn to others in difficult times for a little cheering up after a bad day, or for comfort and help getting through painful experiences. And research has shown that social support is one of the most important protections against depression and anxiety. Those with strong social networks tend to have more resilience and fewer symptoms during rough times.

The paradox is that people who've suffered a trauma often withdraw, just when they need social support the most. It feels safer to them, given the sense of alienation and self-consciousness they have about PTSD. But social isolation enhances their symptoms, and leads to greater feelings of aloneness, despair, and hopelessness.

We also know from research that various parts of the brain are specialized for social behavior and communicating. From the moment we're born, we interact with family members through eye contact, facial expression, sharing new things, laughing together.

Babies that are socially neglected fail to thrive; their brains are underdeveloped. Later in life, they tend to overreact to stress and are prone to depression and anxiety. We continue to need social connection throughout our lives. We know our brains use certain chemicals (i.e., hormones, neurotransmitters) during social interactions. These chemicals promote resilience and help buffer us from stress. Supportive relationships can lower stress hormones such as cortisol, while they raise chemicals such as oxytocin, which enhance feelings of comfort and bonding. That's why positive relationships can be considered social medicine for your social brain, allowing you to reconnect and belong instead of feeling like you're a misunderstood lone survivor.

So how do you overcome the natural social isolation that commonly emerges with PTSD? The path from withdrawal to embracing your relationships involves developing and practicing the eight skills that follow.

Three Tools Necessary for Social Re-Engagement

Before we talk about those eight reconnecting skills, we should review three important tools we introduced in earlier chapters: faking it until you make it; anxiety management and exposure skills; and resisting negative interpretations and mind reading.

Fake it Until You Make It

The first tool—fake it until you make it—was introduced in chapter 5, and is essential for re-establishing social ties. Sometimes you have to do what you don't feel like doing in order to jump-start good feelings and create a new habit. When you begin reaching out to others and engaging socially, it will probably feel to you like you are going through the motions, and it may not seem natural or enjoyable. Being alone can feel more comfortable and safe, while spending time with others takes effort and energy that you think you don't have. It may also bring up some anxiety.

This means that as you start to engage in more social activities, you may have to fight against the tendency to pull back and revert to your old habits. Just remember that after a period of time, your efforts will pay off. The more contact you maintain with others, the easier it will get. Give it time—the enjoyment will grow. If you can hang in there, you will start to re-experience how good it felt to enjoy the company of others.

Anxiety Management and Exposure Skills

One reason people with PTSD withdraw from social activities is trauma-related anxiety and avoidance. Many social activities take place away from the home in a restaurant, coffee shop, club, theater, recreation center, church, or someone else's home. If you have been avoiding such places because of anxiety and panic attacks, undoubtedly your social life has diminished. Some of the exercises in this chapter encourage you to accept invitations to go to lunch or initiate a date with a friend. You'll need to use the anxiety management skills described in chapter 3 as well as the skills for overcoming avoidance in chapter 4 to help you through some of these social activities.

Resist Negative Interpretations and Mind Reading

In chapter 5, we talked about the thinking errors people commonly make when they are depressed, anxious, or angry. There is a strong tendency to assume you know what is going on in someone else's head, and to misread someone's intention toward you as critical, insensitive, or unhelpful. Another common error is to take things personally. Read again the list of negative thinking errors on pages 92–95. You are more likely to make these misinterpretations when you are in a bad mood and feel alienated from others in your life.

It's easy to see how a negative cycle can develop from these thinking errors. You start to reach out to others, but interpret their behavior in negative ways. Let's say you decide to make a special dinner for your spouse, but he or she comes home late from work. You take this personally, and think that because your spouse is late, it means that he or she doesn't want to be around you. This thought alone will make you want to retreat again. If you also get angry and complain, your spouse may become defensive. Now your efforts have turned into an actual conflict, confirming what you feared initially, and undermining your sense of trust and desire to reconnect.

As you begin to reach out more to people and try to expand your social networks, it's important to combat this tendency to misinterpret others. To resist the normal errors in thinking that emerge with anxiety and depression, it's essential that you:

- Regularly review the thinking errors in chapter 5, pages 92–95.

- Try to catch yourself when you automatically misinterpret others' words or deeds, staying open to alternative explanations.

- Listen to what was actually said rather than to your *interpretation* of what was said; give the other person the benefit of the doubt.

- Use the technique to challenge your negative thinking in chapter 5, page 95.

Now that you have your three tools in mind, you can use them as you develop the eight skills for overcoming withdrawal. These skills may seem simple and familiar, yet if you are someone who has retreated from people in your life since the trauma or if you lack an adequate support system, they will make a huge difference in your recovery from PTSD. Just doing them will be its own reward.

Skill 1

Practice "Hanging Out" with Family to Start Connecting

Many people with PTSD withdraw in small but important ways from their families. If you live with a partner, children, parents, or extended-family members, you might be around them every day without being fully present in their lives. One easy way to break this pattern is simply to make a conscious effort to hang out more with them, and find ways to make contact. You may have to overcome an initial habit of withdrawing, but with time it will be easier to socialize. Practice some of these suggestions.

Skill 1 Practice

Hanging Out with Family

- Sit with your family in the den.

- Hire a babysitter so you can spend some time with your spouse or partner.

- If family members are going out to a movie or a meal, go with them.

- Talk to your spouse and kids at dinner.

- Go for a walk with your spouse, child, parent.

- Ask family members about their day, their work, or some project they are working on.

- Act sociable even when you don't feel like it, just for a little while!

These may be small changes in your behavior, but if you've really withdrawn from your family, these suggestions are ways to start reconnecting. You can practice the changes at work or school, too. Hang out in the break room with coworkers instead of taking your lunch alone. Talk with fellow students between classes. Ask someone to have lunch with you at work or school. Make small talk whenever you can—it's good for your social brain!

SKILL 2

Say "Yes" to Invitations to Overcome Withdrawal

People with PTSD often automatically decline social invitations, either from habit or from knowing that accepting will require effort. Invitations may be for a work party, birthday gathering, or dinner with friends, or it may simply be a friend asking you to have coffee, go to the movies, or watch a game together. It's time to start saying yes more often. While it will require effort to muster the energy or overcome any anxiety or self-doubts, remember that this is medicine for your recovery. You don't have to stay for the whole event—small steps to increase contact are great. The key is to start chipping away at the old habits of avoidance, and start opening up your life.

Saying "Yes" to Invitations

- If a friend asks you to go for coffee or the movies, say yes.

- If you or your family get invited to a party or other gathering, go, even if only for a little while.

- If a coworker asks you to lunch, say yes.

- If friends ask you to come play basketball, go biking, or head out for a hike, do it!

- If your partner or spouse wants to do something enjoyable with you, try it.

SKILL 3

Reconnect with Lost Friends to Rebuild Your Network

It's easy to lose touch with friends when you've been through a traumatic experience and are focused on coping with PTSD. Still, your friends were part of your social network; as part of your recovery, you should try to reconnect with them.

You may have to overcome some initial resistance from them. Friends may have initially offered support after the trauma, but if you had difficulty accepting it and pushed them away, they may have felt frustrated and helpless. People in your support system can sometimes withdraw from you if they feel useless, rejected, or unable to help. If, after the trauma, you repeatedly turned down invitations from friends, they probably stopped asking. By now, some time has passed since you talked to them or hung out. You'll need to invite them back.

If you are concerned that friends have withdrawn from you because you were unavailable for a while, you can offer an explanation, saying that you needed some recovery time on your own, or that it was hard to be social at first. At the least, simply acknowledge you've been out of touch. But emphasize the importance of your relationship to them, and take that first step to overcome your isolation. The thing to remember is that the people in your life care about you, and want to feel connected.

SKILL 3 PRACTICE

Steps for Reconnecting with Lost Friends

1. Call, email, or stop by to see the person.

2. Say you know you've been out of touch and less available recently. You can also explain further that it's been a difficult time lately and you haven't wanted to be around people, but now you're ready.

3. Say you'd like to get together for coffee, lunch, a movie, or whatever activities the two of you used to do together.

4. Schedule the date—and keep it!

SKILL 4

Schedule Regular Activities to Create Social Habits

In the beginning, it takes effort and practice to get out of the habit of being alone. One way to give yourself some additional impetus to change is to structure your social contacts by making regular commitments with others. You might want to make a weekly date with a friend for a walk before work, or schedule a regular long-distance call to a friend or relative. Commit to going to the gym with a buddy, or getting your family together once a month for a barbecue.

In chapter 5, we discussed depression and introduced the idea of identifying and scheduling pleasurable activities. If you started a calendar for activity scheduling, take time now to add a regular event to your calendar that involves other people. This might be a weekly walk, going to a religious service each week, or playing sports with a friend on Saturdays. If there is an expectation and a commitment for you to go, you'll be encouraged not to bow out.

Review the social activities on page 104 for additional ideas.

SKILL 4 PRACTICE

Scheduling Regular Social Activities

- Set up a weekly date with a friend to go walking, have coffee, or dinner.

- Make a plan with a friend to play basketball, hike, or go biking once a month.

- Schedule a regular play date with another parent and child.

- Go with a friend or family members to a weekly social event such as a book club, a volunteer group, or a religious service.

- Take a dance or art class with someone.

- Make a weekly plan with a friend to watch Sunday football.

Skill 5
Increase Closeness by Opening Up

So far, we've focused on increasing the amount of contact you have with others. We've encouraged you to hang out more with family, say yes to invitations, seek out lost friends, and to schedule regular social dates to create a consistent pattern of social contact. What we haven't touched on is what you can do to enhance a sense of closeness when you are with someone you have a good connection with. As we mentioned earlier, it is important to avoid mind reading and negative interpretations. What you can do—and it's usually guaranteed to improve your contact with another person—is simply to open up.

We devote a whole chapter—chapter 13—to opening up and talking about your traumatic experience and PTSD. But no matter what you talk about, you can always try to be more open and genuine with people in your life. Most conversations usually include a certain amount of small talk about work, sports, school, or things at home. You always have the option to take the conversation a little deeper by sharing what is truly on your mind and what matters to you. Instead of simply saying "I'm fine" when you're asked, you might answer "I'm feeling a bit down today." Or you might want to share something that touched you this week, or that you're worried about someone in your family.

The idea is to take a risk and be more genuine: Drop the automatic response that "everything is good." Men may find it more difficult to open up in a personal way than women because of social norms, but we encourage you to try. When you open up and share the more personal aspects of your life, both positive and negative, you invite people to step inside your world for a minute.

We should also say that this does not mean you have to launch into a long and detailed conversation about something that's upsetting you. You control how much detail you want to share. Simply acknowledging that you are having a bad day creates a moment of connection, even if you don't say anything else. But if you do want to share more, it's good to check in with the other person ("I'm having a bad day. Do you have a few minutes to talk?"). The other person will usually indicate whether he or she has the time or ability to have a longer conversation with you.

Skill 5 Practice

Increase Closeness by Opening Up

- When talking to others, take a moment to check in with yourself: What am I feeling? What's going on in my life that's important?

- During the course of a conversation, don't just respond automatically that "I'm fine, things are good." Even if it's just a sentence, share something about what's really going on with you.

- Initiate a conversation with a family member or friend about something important in your life (an inspiring moment, ways you are coping with PTSD).

- Seek out someone close to you for a more in-depth talk about something you are struggling with.

Skill 6

Increase Closeness by Giving to Others

It's important to remember that while you may be struggling with PTSD, you still have a lot to give. You may not always feel this way: Many people with PTSD feel useless and helpless much of the time. Some feel like burdens on their families, or that they have nothing to contribute to others. But no matter how significantly trauma has altered your life, you do have something to give. First of all, opening up and being honest with others about what's going on with you is a great way to extend yourself in a relationship. Your open and genuine contact is always a gift to others. But you can also increase closeness by being a good listener, and by offering to help others.

Learning how to be a good listener is essential to relationships, but it's not always obvious or intuitive. The principles of active listening involve encouraging the other person to talk openly about what's troubling him, and being willing to embrace his emotions. This isn't as easy as it sounds: When someone is sad, angry, upset or feeling hopeless, you want to make him feel better by saying things like "It isn't that bad," or "You'll feel better." Or you will want to give him advice or try to solve his problem for him. But usually this feels invalidating to the person who is sharing his emotional pain—the person may sense that you don't accept the way that he feels. Listen and don't try to change the person's feelings or solve the problem; just do your best to empathize. One way to do this is to repeat back what you think he or she is saying or feeling ("Sounds like you're feeling pretty down today"). It's also important to remain supportive: Try to understand from the person's point of view, and resist being judgmental.

If you have PTSD, active listening can be a challenge. Trauma can make you more sensitive to other people's pain, and you may feel like you're already overwhelmed with your own negative emotions. Or you might fear that listening to someone else's hardship will trigger anxiety symptoms in you. Finally, sometimes when friends, coworkers, or family talk about what's stressing them out that day, it can feel trivial compared to what you've been through. These can all get in the way of reaching out and listening to others. You may need to decide when and where you make yourself available to others, and stay alert to your emotional state. If you can do it, give people the room to talk, and be willing to go there with them emotionally even when it's hard. Active, empathetic listening is one of the most powerful gifts you can give another human being.

There are other ways you can give. You can volunteer to do a task or an errand for your spouse, repair a friend's bike, or babysit your neighbor's kids. Giving to others creates a positive feedback loop. On one level, you generate good feelings between you and the person that you're helping. On another level, you see yourself as someone helpful instead of useless, building your confidence and feelings of connectedness. And finally, you are breaking the bad habit of being socially isolated. See chapter 14 for more ideas on ways to contribute to others.

Skill 6 Practice

Increase Closeness by Giving

Give through Active Listening

- Encourage the person to talk, and encourage expression of feelings.

- Be warm, accepting, and nonjudgmental.

- Don't try to diminish his or her distress, or tell the person not to feel the way he or she is feeling.

- Instead, rephrase what you think the person is saying or feeling, so he feels understood.

- Resist the temptation to give advice or solve the person's problem.

Give through Helping

- Offer to help with someone else's kids (pick them up, babysit).

- Offer to make some repairs or do chores for a friend or parent—work on the car or bike, clean out the gutters, fix a piece of furniture.

- Give someone a lift somewhere.

- Save your spouse time by taking over his or her usual job (shopping, cooking, bills).

- Help a friend or child with homework.

- Offer to do research for someone, or use your skills or expertise to provide someone a service.

- See chapter 14 for additional ways to give to family, friends, and your community, or to a cause that helps others.

Identify Your Social Circles to Expand and Deepen Them

People play different roles in your life. Some people you feel very close to. These are the friends and family members you know well and really feel comfortable opening up to and talking with. They are the people you trust and turn to for emotional support in hard times—your "close" circle.

But you also have a broader network of people whom you socialize with in certain settings and groups. These include friends you occasionally spend time with, coworkers, people you play basketball or tennis with, fellow members of any club, association, class or volunteer group you participate in. This circle also includes relatives you see occasionally and neighbors you get together with from time to time. This is your "companionship" network, and it is typically much bigger and broader than your close circle.

A lot has been written about the importance of having someone in your life who provides deep emotional support. This is especially true after trauma, when you are working through very heavy issues; you need people in your close social circle around you. But it's also very important to have people that you can simply enjoy doing things with; your broader social circles can provide this sense of belonging and group identity. Being on a team or a member of a class unites you with other people. Knowing that you are cared about and liked in your local groups or neighborhood helps you feel connected. Having people with whom you can go to lunch or see a performance helps to bring variety and enjoyment into your life.

Take a moment to think about your different social circles. Who fits in your "close" network, and who do you know in your larger "companionship" network? Are you satisfied with your social support in both groups? If you think that you could benefit from expanding and deepening your relationships in either category, there are steps you can take.

Suppose you want to expand your "close" circle. Think about people you know already. Do you know someone in your art class, work group, or soccer team who you would like to get closer to and think would make a good friend? Do you have any friends you occasionally see but could imagine having a more regular and deeper relationship with? If so, then you need to get active and reach out, using the skills in this chapter. Or if you want to expand your companionship network, consider joining coworkers at lunch or becoming part of a new club, group, or team. Increasing your social support and sense of belonging can help you emerge from your PTSD cocoon.

SKILL 7 PRACTICE

Expand Your Social Networks

In your journal, make two lists: the first of the people in your "close" circle, and the second of the people in your "companions and group membership" circle.

Examine Your "Close" Circle

- Take a look at your close circle and decide if you want to add people to this network.

- If the answer is yes, identify an existing friend, relative, coworker, or individual in your companions list that you might want to cultivate as a closer friend.

- Reach out and make a date to have coffee or lunch. Use the other skills in this chapter to slowly deepen the relationship.

Examine Your "Companionship" Circle

- Take a look at your companions and group membership list, and decide if you want to expand this network.

- If the answer is yes, join a book club, political organization, sports team, volunteer group, professional association, or social group at work.

SKILL 8

Enrich Your Partner Relationship by Rekindling Romance

If you have a spouse or partner, you may have noticed that PTSD can take the spontaneity and romance right out of your relationship. Recovering from trauma is a painful process that's often filled with anxiety and depression, and coping with PTSD takes time, energy, and courage. There's usually very little left over for romance. But remember the theme of this chapter: Although reaching out to others takes some work, if you are able to get things rolling, the rewards to your health, happiness, and well-being are worth it! The same is true for the intimate side of your relationship. And small efforts can make a big difference, especially if you try something special each week to deepen your love.

Rekindling Romance

- Surprise your partner with a small romantic gift: Bring home a favorite dessert, flowers, or something else he or she would like.

- If you have kids, hire a sitter and have a date night once or twice a month.

- Take time one evening or morning to make love; try to slowly increase the frequency of your sexual activity.

- Go out for a romantic meal, movie, or show.

- Surprise your spouse with a romantic dinner at home.

- Write your partner a card telling him or her something you admire or love about him, or simply that you love her.

- Go on a walk, and take a picnic lunch with you.

- Be affectionate: Hold hands, sit close when you are watching television, give spontaneous hugs or kisses.

- Do something new or unusual together. Visit a nearby town; rent bikes on the beach; ride a rollercoaster; drive to a hill or mountain top and watch the sunset.

Moving Forward

When you begin reaching out to others and engaging socially, it may not feel natural or enjoyable at first. If you are used to keeping to yourself or have retreated from companionship after the trauma, spending time with others may feel like a difficult task—you will have to fight against the tendency to pull back. But connecting with others is absolutely essential to healing, so make the effort and take your social medicine. If you can start doing some of the activities suggested in this chapter, you will find that you will feel more supported in your life, and your enjoyment will grow.

CHAPTER 9

From Explode to Explain

Nicole

Nicole was quick to anger her whole life. She knew this was how she coped with her abuse: Better to confront than to be taken advantage of. She looked for signs of dishonesty or manipulation in others, and when she felt hurt by someone's actions, she had difficulty giving the person the benefit of the doubt. She also liked the righteous feeling of confronting someone during a conflict, because it proved she was no longer a weak child. Nicole could see that her reactions were driving her apart from Peter, her fiancé. Her anger focused on the ways he seemed to be detaching from her, which only made things worse. But she had difficulty reining in her anger, and did not know how to reach him.

Dan

Dan was mad about everything when he got back from Iraq. He was angry that he had been redeployed after being at home such a short time, that the troops didn't have good equipment to protect them-selves, and that he was "so screwed up" because of his experience there. He took offense whenever friends who hadn't served talked about the war. When he started drinking more, his fights with his wife, Heather, got worse, usually ending with screaming matches. He felt out of control and alienated from her and everyone else in his life. Recently, Heather had threatened to move out, and Dan panicked. He didn't know why he was angry so much of the time—or what to do about it.

Anger is common in people who have experienced trauma. It is partly physiological: People with PTSD have an overactive alarm system, and the surges of stress hormones and adrenalin can increase irritability. Anger can also be a reasonable response to the trauma itself—to being attacked, seeing others die in war or a dis-aster, having to kill others in the line of duty, or feeling powerless to help others or defend yourself. Anger is often fueled by the sense that others do not understand your trauma experience. They can't imagine what it was like to survive an earthquake or become dis-abled in a motorcycle accident. Finally, anger is an emotion that can feel very empowering, which is quite alluring for trauma survivors who often feel weak, helpless, or estranged.

The problem with anger is that it's usually aimed at those you are close to, and it can significantly interfere with your relation-ships. In the previous chapter, we talked about the importance of social support and connections in recovering from PTSD, and gave you strategies to overcome tendencies to withdraw from people. In this chapter, you'll learn how anger may be driving a wedge between you and others, and how to resolve conflicts with loved ones.

You do have a choice between expressing your anger spontaneously, without censorship, or channeling it into constructive behaviors that help rather than hurt your relationships. To transform your anger from outbursts to effective communication that fosters conflict resolution, we'll give you a six-step strategy:

- Step 1: Take time out to regain control and think.

- Step 2: Resist the anger traps.

- Step 3: Identify your underlying feelings and needs.

- Step 4: Communicate your feelings and needs.

- Step 5: Listen and empathize with the other person.

- Step 6: Make a request and work collaboratively.

Before we get to the steps, you need to understand why it's so easy to get angry, the emotions that anger usually masks, and the reasons you may want to rein in your anger to better address your needs and resolve conflicts.

What Triggers Anger?

Emotions play an important role for human beings. They signal that we have interpreted a situation in a particular way, and the resulting emotion motivates certain behaviors.

We've talked a lot about how anxiety is part of our alarm response to *perceived danger*, as it gears the body up for fight or flight in response to a threat. Anger is a response to *perceived harm*. It follows an automatic thought that someone is trying to hurt or mistreat you.

Thought	Emotion	Behavior
That person is following me (danger)	fear/anxiety	escape or get inside
She is intentionally ignoring me (mistreatment)	anger	cold shoulder or confront

Notice that when we talk about anger, we say *perceived* mistreatment. All of our emotional reactions are responses to *the way we interpret events*, whether that interpretation is accurate or not. It's the idea we discussed in chapter 5—anxiety or sadness can sometimes be a response to an automatic thought that isn't accurate. Because first interpretations can be misguided, it is very important to take time to evaluate your perception.

Why People Like Anger

One of the most important—and briefly satisfying—aspects of anger is that it is an energizing and empowering response to a challenge. Anger activates the same physiological alarm system as the one triggered by anxiety we described in chapter 3 (including the fast sympathetic adrenalin response and the slower cortisol response). These physical changes prepare you for action—the fight-or-flight response. Your breathing increases to bring in more oxygen, your body starts converting stored energy into glucose to raise your blood-sugar level, and your heart starts pumping to move that oxygenated blood and fuel to your muscles.

But unlike anxiety (or most other emotions), anger also creates a sense of strength and control. Instead of being helpless, misused, or weak, you are the one on the move—defending yourself, confronting your attacker, insisting upon fair treatment, righting a wrong. Indeed, when people are angry, they feel righteous and justified in their behavior. Sometimes this is an appropriate stance, but often anger involves misinterpreting others' intentions.

No matter what the reality, anger is often experienced in the moment as positive, because you feel empowered and protected in your response. That's why Dan always felt better when he was angry than when he felt hurt, sad, or anxious. Yet, anger can often disguise what is really going on with you.

Because Anger Feels Empowering, It Often Masks Other Feelings

Anger can hide feelings of vulnerability—and no one likes to feel vulnerable. If you just broke up with someone, it's so much easier to get angry than to feel sad about the breakup, which would be natural. If your spouse tailgates another car while driving, you will feel more powerful if you yell at him or her instead of simply saying that his or her driving is making you anxious.

When you get angry, you have the sense that anger will get the result you want, though this usually isn't true. When Nicole and Peter fight and he withdraws to another room, on the surface Nicole feels indignant and mistreated, but underneath she fears that he doesn't care about her. There are vulnerable feelings underneath the anger she displays as she walks by and slams the door. Those feelings are emotional pain related to not feeling loved, and anxiety about whether she and Peter will be able to make their relationship work. Anger between people in close relationships usually surfaces around issues of feeling rejected, criticized, or ignored—in other words, not feeling respected or cared about. It's better to talk about these deeper feelings, which shift the focus to you (how you are feeling) and away from the other person (the blame game). More on that below!

Anger can also be an expression of anxiety, which is why it's so often associated with PTSD. When you face a sniper attack during combat or are threatened by an ex-boyfriend, remember that the same physiological alarm system is activated for both anxiety and anger. Sometimes you may have to stay and fight, defending yourself if you can't escape.

Men may be more likely to respond to a threat with anger rather than anxiety. When Dan came home from Iraq, he grew anxious every time he rode the bus to work. One morning, when the bus was particularly crowded, a man unintentionally pressed up against him. Dan's fear was triggered—in Iraq, this contact might easily have signaled an attack. His alarm system cranked into high gear and so did his anger: He shoved the man hard, causing him to fall and other passengers to respond with shock and fear. Even in less scary situations, the physiological symptoms of anxiety can cause people with PTSD to be irritable and to explode easily at others.

What Are the Costs of Anger?

In the moment, anger may feel better than sadness, hurt, anxiety, or shame, but there are some high costs. Your relationships suffer, your real feelings and needs do not get addressed, and your health is compromised.

The most obvious downside to anger is the way it damages relationships. Anger rarely achieves its goal of setting something right or getting a need met. Instead, it creates the opposite reaction and blocks any hope of collaboration. You know this from times when you've been the target of someone's anger: Instantly, you're on the defensive, which makes it very difficult to listen and work through the problem. So when you're acting angry, you can be sure the other person isn't listening to your point of view. What you want from them—understanding, reassurance, reconnection—is not going to happen if you are yelling or criticizing. Anger that is not managed constructively is also harmful because it generally sets off an escalating game of blaming, criticism, insults, and character assassination. At its worst, anger can drive couples and families apart and undermine trust and good will. Both Dan and Nicole could see how their anger might destroy their relationships if they didn't find a better way to cope with the PTSD and communicate what they needed.

Although anger can make you feel powerful, many people find that they cross the line into going out of control. Dan feared his own rage, and felt great shame that he had shoved an innocent man on the bus—and that he might do something similar in the future. Especially for veterans, anger has been an inherent part of combat operations, providing motivation to do battle and helping them to survive. Anger was adaptive in war; at home, it is not.

Anger can also have significant health effects, raising blood pressure and increasing the risk of heart attacks and strokes. Anger is associated with headaches, muscle tension, increased pain, and stomach and intestinal problems.

The Steps from Explode to Explain to Resolve!

If anger does not address your needs or grievances, but hurts your relationships with others, you may be open to finding a more effective way to communicate and resolve conflicts. If so, we invite you learn these six steps, and practice them often with friends and family members. They will make a huge difference in your life and your recovery from trauma.

Take a Time Out to Regain Composure

If you take away only one anger-management strategy from this chapter, this should be it. The idea of taking a time out may seem silly if you associate it with punishing kids, but we're talking about a slightly different technique. With kids, time outs teach them to control themselves; with adults, you teach yourself.

> *Taking a time out is the most important thing to do when you are angry.*

Once your heart starts pumping and your brain is flooded with adrenalin, you can't force yourself to calm down. Your fists will clench, your tone will become harsh, threatening, or sarcastic, and you will be incapable of conducting a reasonable conversation. When you feel harmed, you have the urge to strike back. With rage surging, you may well inflame the situation into an even bigger confrontation. To avoid an escalating conflict, you must step away from the situation to collect yourself. Try saying, "I want to talk to you later about this, but I need to take a break and cool down." Then leave. Do not return until the surge of anger has died down.

A time out is necessary to give your brain and body time to cool down. It's that simple. Even five or ten minutes can make a big difference in regaining your composure; if you're really angry, we suggest taking an hour or even longer. The time out period is intended for you to do whatever it takes to calm down—go for a walk, watch television, take a bath, read the paper. Whatever you do, you should actively resist the temptation to review what just happened to you. On the heels of a fight, your mind will typically want to think about how the other person wronged you. Ruminating over the episode is a mental strategy that we naturally employ so we feel like we aren't losing control or being dominated. Unfortunately, rumination invariably keeps anger alive. When you notice yourself ruminating, just try to think of anything else and do something that settles you. Once you are calmer, approach the person as an ally who wants to resolve the conflict.

STEP 1 PRACTICE

Take a Time Out

- When you notice that you're getting really angry during a conversation, STOP.

- Tell the other person you want to take time to cool down so that you can talk about the issue later when you aren't so angry.

- Do an activity that helps you feel more settled.

- Do not think about the conflict until you feel calmer.

- When you are ready, approach the person again and move to steps 2 through 6, below.

STEP 2

Resist the Anger Traps

People don't think or act in a fair, balanced, or reasonable way when they are angry. The world becomes black or white, the person you are fighting with becomes the enemy, and the focus is on winning through any means.

This tendency to see things in the extreme and make the other person the bad guy is similar to the thought errors that we talked about in chapter 5. Just as depression tends to make people assign negative interpretations to events, anger has its own set of distortions. Powerful moods always involve chemical changes in the brain that shift our thinking. The anger state of mind is a hard one to escape once you are engaged in a fight; that's why the first step is always a time out. If you don't take that break, your anger will drive you to do many impulsive, harmful behaviors such as yelling, criticizing, blaming, swearing, and hurling insults—and the conflict will snowball.

Below are common anger traps. When you feel yourself getting angry, *notice these traps and resist them*—90 percent of the battle is simply awareness. When you see that you are starting to blame or make character judgments, stop talking and check in with yourself. If you already feel pretty angry, take a time out. If your feelings are still fairly mild and you can look at your own behavior, try to identify your anger trap.

1. **Urgency.** When you are angry, you have the urge to regain a sense of power and control immediately. You feel you have to correct the offending behavior right away—it can't wait. But this is a trap. You wind up venting at the person, and your outburst invariably makes him or her feel attacked and defensive. Don't act when you are really angry. Bite your tongue. Take a time out to give your anger a chance to clear so you can begin to resolve the conflict.

2. **Mind reading ill intent.** When you're angry or hurt, you have a tendency to interpret the other person's behavior as intentionally neglectful, mean, harmful, or disrespect-

ful. If a friend hasn't called you in months, you think, "She's purposely ignoring me. She must be annoyed with me." You assume you know what's in her head, and that she is punishing you in a passive way (intentionally ignoring you to communicate her displeasure). You probably don't consider more neutral alternatives (she's busy; its not personal). When someone has hurt you, it's natural to believe it was intentional ("Why didn't he stop himself if he didn't really mean to attack me?"). But this type of thinking is just a way to mentally protect ourselves. Most of the time, others harm us inadvertently or out of self-defense, not from a conscious intent to injure us.

3. **Blaming.** Blame is automatic. When you are angry, you are always *angry at someone.* You focus on how others hurt or wronged you in some way. It's their fault. As your level of anger increases, your focus lands on the other person's behavior ("the best defense is a good offense" reflex). And because thoughts and feelings become exaggerated when you are angry, it often feels very black or white: You are blameless, while the other person has transgressed in some extreme, shocking way. You don't think about your role or contribution. You focus only on them, probably assuming they intended to hurt you, and you're ready to convict them without a trial or jury. This is why you feel justified in lecturing, yelling, giving them the cold shoulder, or storming out.

4. **Self-righteousness.** There is also something about anger that makes people feel, "I'm right, he's wrong." Righteousness is the complement to blame: The other person

is at fault (blame), and therefore you are right and justi-fied in responding however you see fit. Anger often comes with a feeling of moral superiority and offense that the other person treated you in such an unfair man-ner. If you've labeled your housemate as a slob, you see yourself in contrast as the responsible, considerate one. Righteousness is another black or white way of seeing the conflict.

5. **Exaggerated thoughts and feelings.** As your anger rises, your feelings and interpretations become more extreme. If your spouse forgets something at the store, you say to him or her, "You NEVER remember!" You don't just feel annoyed; you're really ticked off. Or if a friend is late picking you up, you think, "She doesn't care about me! Why are we even going to coffee?" Whatever you are thinking becomes all or nothing, your emotion goes off the meter. When you're having this reaction, it is impor-tant to remember that these extreme thoughts are how the angry mind tries to gain control and take the offen-sive. Catch yourself thinking them and resist the "never" or "always" comments.

6. **Character judgments.** Going right along with black or white exaggerations is the tendency to take a behavior (your partner didn't clean the kitchen this week) and turn it into a global character trait (she's a slob, he's irre-sponsible). If you've been fighting with your friend lately, you start to think, "She's a pretty selfish person" instead of sticking to the specific situation, behavior, or conflict. Anger pulls you to make judgmental characterizations

about the person, instead of focusing on the behavior (which he or she might be willing to change in a collaborative negotiation). Negatively labeling someone's character is an act of disrespect that will drive him or her further away.

Resist the Anger Traps

- Resist anger's urgency: Wait to talk or act until you are settled.

- Don't assume that you know what the other person is thinking.

- Leave open the possibility the person you are angry with may not have intended you any harm, even if you are hurt.

- Remind yourself that thoughts and feelings are more extreme when you are angry.

- Keep your focus on behavior; don't make character judgments or label others.

- Resist blaming.

- Resist righteousness. Strive for empathy, respect, and having faith in the other person.

STEP 3

Identify Your Underlying Feelings and Needs

The first two steps above are intended to help you slow down and stop your initial response of blaming, criticizing, and yelling. This is no easy feat, we know: Anger floods your body with adrenalin, distorts your interpretations, and urges you to act on impulse. That's why it's so important to stop the escalation and step back, calm down, and start thinking. Once you've settled down, shift your focus from the other person to *you*. It's important to figure out what feelings and needs lie beneath your anger, so you can communicate what you really want in the relationship and work out a solution that may actually satisfy some of your needs.

Trying to identify all of your feelings when you are angry is a challenge. Recall that you will want to feel and express anger instead of hurt or anxiety, because anger activates you and makes you feel more in control, powerful, and righteous. But in relationships, anger is usually a mask for something else.

All human beings have needs to feel close, accepted, cared for, respected, and valued. What is usually lurking below the surface of anger is a *perceived threat* to these needs. We want to emphasize *perceived*, because how you interpret a volatile situation may not be entirely accurate, though your feelings will follow naturally from your interpretation of what's going on.

Let's say your spouse calls your dinner plans off for the fifth time this month, because he or she must work late. Your automatic angry reaction may be that he or she is self-centered. But what's underneath that? What you can be sure of is that you have *a need to feel close* to your spouse, and you *fear* that he or she may be more interested in work than in spending time with you. What is true is that you were *hurt* when he or she cancelled, although you cannot be sure if you are interpreting your spouse's behavior accurately. Anger is usually a subjective experience of not feeling close or valued, or fearing that the person in your life may be withdrawing his or her love. But you need to check in with the other person about his or her thoughts and experience: First, share your fears and desires, then listen (that's step 4).

Nicole was only aware of her rage at Peter when they would fight, but not of her underlying feelings. Sometimes, he'd give her a spontaneous hug. She'd bristle because the hug was unexpected, and she was still getting comfortable with various forms of affection. An exasperated Peter would sigh, say nothing more, and withdraw to read his paper. That's when Nicole would explode: "I've told you a hundred times not to hug me that way because of my past! And now you just sit there in a huff!"

What's going on here? Nicole has a need to feel safe in this relationship, and she had explained to Peter what would help—no surprise hugs. But she really got angry when he retreated behind his newspaper, because withdrawing during a conflict—not asking for a time out, but simply cutting off communication—can be perceived as either intentional punishment or rejection. For Nicole, Peter's withdrawal triggered a fear that she might lose him because of her PTSD, and that she might never be able to have a committed relationship. These are the vulnerable feelings underneath Nicole's anger: feeling emotionally abandoned in the moment and fearing that Peter may someday stop caring for her. For Peter, Nicole's sudden and negative response to his hug felt like rejection. Deep down, he worried that she might never trust him and let him in. His self-protective withdrawal unintentionally escalated the fight.

Identify Your Underlying Feelings and Needs

- Take time to explore whatever feelings you may have underneath your anger (are you hurt, sad, disappointed, or anxious?).

- Try to identify whether these feelings are related to the perception or fear that some important need in your relationship may be threatened:

  - You may be thinking, "He/she doesn't care about me."

  - You may be thinking, "I'm not important to him or her anymore."

  - You may be thinking, "He/she is going to leave me."

  - You may be thinking, "He/she doesn't value or respect me."

- Keep in mind that your interpretation of what's going on with the other person may not be accurate.

STEP 4

Communicate Your Feelings and Needs

Once you understand what's really going on with you, you're in a position to communicate your feelings and needs clearly. The way to do this is to let the other person know what your experience was: how you interpreted what he or she did, and why you felt hurt, disappointed, or anxious. You want to explain your reaction, without assuming that your perception is necessarily the truth. You will be checking in with the other person's reality in step 5.

In Nicole's case, she might tell Peter that she still has an automatic, negative response to unexpected physical contact, and she still needs him to be careful about how he expresses affection as she works through issues with her sexual abuse. She might offer to try not to bristle or react negatively, but instead just gently remind him not to touch her unexpectedly if it happens again. Nicole also needs to talk about how she feels when Peter withdraws, how painful it is when he pulls away, and her fears about the relationship. Peter would then explain why he withdraws, and his need to also feel that they have a close and trusting relationship.

Notice that the focus stays on you: your feelings, your needs, your behavior. It is never positive or effective to focus on the other person's behavior through criticizing, blaming, vilifying, or making extreme and probably unfair comments. One communication strategy that is often recommended, to help you talk from your perspective and not accuse the other, is to use "I" statements. Nicole would say: "I feel suddenly afraid when you touch me and I'm not expecting it," then explain further what she means. Then she should talk about her deeper fears about the relationship: "I feel hurt when you withdraw—I'm afraid you are emotionally withdrawing more and more each day, and that you might leave me."

Communicating your needs is also a great opening to apologize if you said something during the conflict that was mean, unfair, or which you regret. Apologizing is hard, because even if you are aware of your part in a conflict, your instinct is still to keep your guard up and try to control the other person. In these situations, making an apology feels like you are showing your jugular vein and giving the other person permission to continue to harm you. But on the contrary, apologizing for your own misbehavior is one of the very best things you can do. It is a way of being more open, honest, and collaborative. It makes the other person feel far less defensive, and better able to hear what you are trying to communicate. Try it-you'll be surprised at the positive outcome!

STEP 4 PRACTICE

Communicate Your Feelings and Needs

- Use "I" statements to keep the focus on your perspective and not the other person's behavior.

- Describe what you are feeling beneath the anger (hurt, sad, disappointed, small, unimportant, abandoned, or anxious).

- Explain what's important to you in the relationship.

- Explain how you felt in the situation, what important needs of yours felt threatened.

- Emphasize that your interpretation of what happened may not be completely accurate, and that you want the other person to explain his or her experience too.

- Apologize for anything you did in the conflict (such as falling into one of the anger traps).

Listen and Empathize with the Other Person

The next step in managing anger and resolving a conflict is to actively listen to the other person, and to try to put yourself in his or her shoes. This is a challenge because you usually trust your own interpretations. You assume he or she did something wrong—why else would you be so angry? Being open-minded is an act of courage because it may make you feel like you are less protected, and you want your defenses up. Nevertheless, chances are that your interpretations are skewed or exaggerated. Almost everyone's are during a fight.

Each person has a unique experience in a conflict or situation, and it's usually harmful to try to identify what the objective reality is. Often, both people are reacting in a way that makes some sense if you could look at things from their perspectives. And you both want to feel understood. So how can you step inside his or her shoes for a moment and really listen? Encourage the other person to talk, listen closely without judgment, and don't interrupt. Ask him to explain what his experience of the conflict is, what was going on in his head, how he might have been misinterpreting you, and what he needs from you. It's helpful to paraphrase or summarize what the other person said, to be sure you understand and to let him know that you are really trying. And always, try to empathize with what it might have felt like to be the other person in the situation. You will find that this can be one of the most powerful ways to defuse a conflict and engender positive understanding.

Listen and Empathize

- Encourage the person to explain what was happening for him or her during the conflict.

- Don't interrupt, even if what he say feels inaccurate or unfair; you can address these issues when the person is finished.

- See if you can rephrase what you think the other person is saying or feeling so he or she feels understood.

- Strive to put yourself in the other person's shoes to really empathize with his or her experience.

STEP 6

Make a Request and Work Collaboratively

Because conflicts usually emerge around needs that feel threatened or unmet, it's important to work out some kind of agreement or solution. It may be that your primary goal is simply mutual understanding. If this is what you really want, steps 4 and 5 will get you there.

But frequently, you or both parties have additional goals— things you would like to ask for. You should make your request specific and behavior-oriented ("Would you be willing to wash the dishes once or twice a week?" instead of "Stop being a slob!"). Nicole can request that if Peter is angry, he should talk to her about it instead of withdrawing in silence. He might suggest a compromise, telling her that he's taking a time out with the newspaper but will reconnect with her in 20 or 30 minutes. Peter might ask Nicole not to make exaggerated or harsh statements ("I've told you a thousand times . . .").

We call such statements "requests" because you always have the right to your feelings and needs, but you do not have an inherent right to require that someone fulfill them. You can make a request, with the recognition that the other person may say yes or no, or seek some type of compromise. Asking once is essential; asking repeatedly means that *you* may simply want your own way and may not be willing to compromise.

This is what it means to be assertive. It is the healthy middle ground between being passive (not talking about your feelings or needs) and aggressive (forcing your interpretation on the other, insisting that the other person do what you want). Assertiveness involves clearly communicating your feelings and desires, while respecting the other person's boundaries. Assertiveness is not a matter of making demands, threats, or bullying the other person. Remember that the other person has needs too, and will likely have his or her own requests. It never hurts to offer to make your own changes when you make a request. While you can't control whether or not the other person will agree to your request, you can at least communicate it in a way that will make collaboration and understanding much more likely.

Making a Request and Working Collaboratively

- Identify your goal in the conflict; it should be related to your feelings and needs that are identified above.

- Request a specific behavioral change that will help achieve that goal, but allow the other person the right to say yes, no, or offer a counterproposal.

- Be willing to negotiate a compromise if the other person does not agree.

- Offer to make a change yourself.

- Try to formulate a mutual agreement.

Moving Forward

When you are angry with someone important in your life, remember what your ultimate goals are for the relationship and for resolving the conflict. If you are really honest with yourself, chances are that your goal is not to vent, lash out, or vilify. This will drive your friend, family member, or partner even further away. Your goal is usually to feel understood and cared for, and to be closer to those people in your life. Strive to act in ways you can feel good about, regardless of how the other person is acting. Even when you have been hurt, try to treat yourself and the other person with respect, empathy, and value.

SECTION 5

From Trauma
to Growth

CHAPTER 10

How Trauma Challenges Your Beliefs

Angela

Before Hurricane Katrina, Angela was a confident and vivacious woman who could bring people together with her vision. She was a natural leader, who combined determination, enthusiasm, and humor in a way that motivated others. But after she lost her home and mother to the hurricane, her view of herself and the world darkened. Life felt fragile and precarious; Angela lost her confidence. She no longer had a sense of drive, faith, or purpose. Eventually, she found her way again, but not until she started trying to understand how her traumatic experience had undermined her belief systems, and left her struggling in uncharted territory.

■

Ian

Ian lived a predictable and comfortable life before he was assaulted. He had his network of college friends in New York, and felt he had found a career in computer programming that suited him. But after his confrontation with the men who stole his car, feelings of terror and vulnerability took over. As his PTSD symptoms worsened, he felt increasingly weak and helpless. He had difficulty relating to friends and coworkers, and his programming work seemed meaningless now. At the age of twenty-six, he didn't know who he was anymore; the future seemed bleak and without promise.

Trauma can profoundly disrupt your deeply held beliefs about yourself, other people, and the world. These core beliefs are how you make sense of your life. They guide your behavior in various situations, and help you navigate relationships and plan for the future. But because a trauma is so unexpected, terrifying, and extreme, it often violates your belief systems. Trauma can threaten your fundamental sense of safety in the world, and weaken your sense of control over your life. You may find normal life meaningless and trivial, blame yourself for what happened, or start to distrust others. These changes in core beliefs in response to the trauma can shake your self-esteem, interfere with your ability to have relationships, and change how you live your life.

But there is a way through this. The key is to understand how your beliefs have changed, and whether you have adopted new beliefs that may feel self-protective but are in reality extreme and harmful. Then you can work to revise your beliefs in a more balanced way, integrating the trauma into healthier beliefs about yourself, your loved ones, and the world. Ultimately this can lead you to grow in new and profound ways, which we'll talk about more in chapter 13.

How Core Beliefs Ground You

All human beings have core beliefs about who they are, what other people are like, and the nature of the world. These beliefs help you to understand and predict what you and others will do and how things should unfold in your life.

For example, your core beliefs about your friends may be that they should possess qualities such as honesty and loyalty, while your core beliefs about what supervisors are like in the workplace might be that they are generally self-centered or incompetent. In your beliefs about how the world works, you may think that events are not random or that only bad people commit violence. Your self-beliefs include basic characteristics of your personality and behavior, for instance that you are quiet, helpful, somewhat temperamental, devoted to family, and so on. All of these fundamental beliefs give you a sense of order, predictability, and control in the world. They guide your behavior and your relationships with others. They ground you in your life.

How Trauma Undermines Your Core Beliefs

Because trauma is usually an unexpected and deeply disturbing experience that contradicts your existing beliefs about yourself, others, or the world, it severely disrupts your core beliefs. For example, you may believe that strangers commit acts of violence, not close friends or family members. If your spouse beats you up during a fight, however, you have to reconcile this contradiction. You must either deny the reality of the trauma ("It wasn't abuse—he lost control," or "It was my fault") in order to preserve your core belief, or you must change your belief to incorporate the new information ("Those I love are capable of violence").

A common conviction that people have is the just-world belief: Bad things happen to bad people, and good things happen to good people. This belief helps people feel safe—if you are kind, responsible, hard working, and devout, bad things won't happen to you or your family. But if your town was devastated by a tornado, you are forced to face the reality that the world can be unjust, even if you are a good person.

When the reality of the trauma shatters your assumptions, you are usually left in a state of confusion and denial. Remember that your core beliefs are the way you understand everything in your life. Traumas can be deeply disorienting in this way, especially in the beginning. You may not even be aware of this mental struggle. You are simply left floating in a world that no longer makes sense or feels predictable. But eventually you will try to make sense of what happened, which generally involves changing your beliefs to incorporate the reality of the trauma.

New Extreme Beliefs Can Interfere with Recovery

Because a trauma is such a profoundly frightening and unexpected experience, it is natural to want to make sure it doesn't happen again. Since your former beliefs couldn't help you anticipate the danger, there is a strong instinctual pull to adjust your beliefs in order to prevent a reoccurrence. Your brain does this by *automatically adopting more extreme beliefs*. People with PTSD develop new core beliefs such as "Men can't be trusted" or "The world isn't a safe place," in order to make sure they are never caught off-guard again.

But these extreme, self-protective beliefs can interfere with your long-term recovery from PTSD. They wall you off from yourself and from other people. They constrict your activities and keep you constantly on alert for danger. They rob you of pleasure and joy in the world and undermine your spirituality. These extreme beliefs can also become a habitual and self-defeating way of interpreting events, keeping you trapped in a world that seems perpetually threatening.

When PTSD alters your beliefs in this way, there is only one thing to do to aid your recovery and restore a more fulfilling life: Revise your convictions about the world. While this may seem scary (e.g., to start trusting some people), you will learn that the potential risk, loss, or pain is not all-or-nothing. You can endure small risks in order to get your life back.

Revising Your Beliefs in a Healthy Way

Since PTSD naturally leads to overly self-protective and self-defeating beliefs, you need to find a healthier way to think. This doesn't mean denying what happened in the trauma, but rather integrating it into a new way of seeing the world. It is essential to identify what has truly been lost (and grieve that loss), what you have learned about yourself (strengths and weaknesses), and whether there is a new but nourishing perspective that might come out of your experience (such as acknowledging the fragility of life, but using this to prioritize what really matters). These honest and realistic changes need to replace the exaggerated and damaging beliefs that may feel protective, but actually perpetuate your suffering.

The following sections are designed to help you explore how your core beliefs have changed as a result of the trauma, and, if some of your beliefs are extreme and unrealistic, to revise them so they are more balanced and healthy. These core beliefs tend to fall into several categories:

- Safety

- Power and Control

- Self Esteem

- Relationships

- World, Faith, and Life Purpose

Because many people with PTSD try to avoid thinking about their trauma and how it has affected them, this may be new terrain for you. But remember as you work through these sections that the process of mentally integrating your trauma experience into your life is essential to your healing.

Working through Beliefs about Safety

Because trauma threatens the physical or emotional integrity of the survivor, people with PTSD find that their sense of safety has been shattered. Life suddenly feels unpredictable and dangerous. Before, you probably felt fairly safe in your life. After the trauma, however, you may feel that you—and those you care about—are not protected from bad things happening. If your trauma involved interpersonal violence, then you may see other people as dangerous too (see beliefs about relationships, listed below).

After the car accident, Sonya was haunted by the feeling that no one was safe, that she or anyone she loved could die at any moment. Not only did she avoid getting in cars, she became obsessed with protecting her son, Eric, rarely letting him out of her sight. After returning from Iraq, Dan also felt vulnerable in a way that was new to him. He developed a new core belief that violence is random and can come from anywhere, so he must always be on alert. Both Sonya and Dan felt that some traumatic end would shorten their futures. Here are some of their beliefs that developed following their traumas, which they were able to identify through therapy and writing:

- No one is really safe, ever.

- I or a loved one can die at any moment.

- Violence is random and can happen anywhere.

- Accidents are unpredictable and can happen any time.

- I will not live a long life.

- Even people who look safe are potentially very dangerous.

Step 1: What Are Your Beliefs about Safety Since the Trauma?

Identify and write down your own beliefs about safety that have developed as a result of your trauma in your journal.

Step 2: Challenge Your Safety Beliefs

Are your post-trauma beliefs about safety balanced and accurate? Often, new safety beliefs are extreme in order to be highly protective: If you now believe that you are never safe, you will never let down your guard. Such an all-or-nothing belief makes you feel less vulnerable. Instead, ask yourself whether you need to be vigilant all the time. Extreme beliefs generally are not an accurate assessment of reality. They also motivate behaviors that bring with them a high cost, such as constant anxiety and avoidance. For instance, the statement, "I or someone I love can die at any moment," is technically true; in reality, however, most people don't die unexpectedly. Sonya's and Dan's close calls have made it seem to them as if this possibility was likely to happen to them imminently. But it's important to put even one's own experience into perspective, and understand that just because a belief evokes strong anxiety, that doesn't make it more real.

Take a look at what you wrote in your journal about feeling unsafe in the world. Are any of your statements examples of all-or-nothing thinking? You might want to review the common thinking errors in chapter 5 (pages 92–95) and think about whether the beliefs you have developed since the trauma are extreme and perhaps not accurate.

Again, it is understandable why you feel so unsafe—the symptoms of anxiety make you feel as if you are in constant danger, and no one wants to repeat a trauma. But we'd like you to take a moment to reflect upon these changes. Consider also examples that might modify the belief so that it is not black or white. For example, Sonya believes that no one is ever safe. But are there ever times when Sonya does feel safe? When she thought about it, she realized that she feels safe at home when Eric is sleeping. She also could see that some situations are riskier than others (riding a bike in traffic is a higher risk than sitting at home reading; walking alone in a dangerous neighborhood at night is riskier than grocery shopping during the day). In other words, safety varies with the situation—Sonya is not in significant danger all of the time.

This is the procedure for challenging your safety beliefs:

- Consider whether your beliefs seem extreme (black or white).

- Try to come up with examples that show gradations of risk.

- Think about other evidence that suggests your belief may be extreme and not realistic.

Step 3: Consider What May Be True about Your Belief

Not all of your beliefs will necessarily be unrealistic. It's important to identify any kernel of truth in a given belief, in order to revise it in a way that is more accurate and balanced, which you'll do in step 4 below. For example, Sonya did experience a serious car accident. In the United States, motor vehicle accidents account for 119 deaths daily. You are not entirely safe on the roads, and it's wise to remember that. Yet, your risk is only one in two-and-a-half *million* of being killed in an auto accident on any given day. If Sonya can incorporate the minimal likelihood of an accident or another traumatic event into her new beliefs about safety, she will have put the potential danger into perspective.

But that's often the really hard part about post-traumatic stress. Most people with PTSD don't want to have any risk at all. Even one chance in two-and-a-half million seems too much if it means there is even the slightest possibility of the trauma recurring. To overcome PTSD, you will not only need to more accurately assess the possibility of danger, but to change your willingness to tolerate small risks in order to live your life fully.

Step 4: Revise Your Beliefs Regarding Safety

Now that you have examined your beliefs about safety and considered what is true and what may be extreme, try to revise your beliefs regarding safety so they are more accurate and balanced.

Working through Beliefs about Being in Control

Along with feeling that the world is unsafe, many trauma survivors find that their beliefs about how much control they have over their lives also change. You may feel that you cannot protect yourself or those you love from harm. You are up against forces that are more powerful than you—war, terrorism, natural disaster, crime, serious illness. It may feel as if it makes no difference if you work hard, try to help others, or do the morally right thing: You lack the power to control events.

People with PTSD also experience a loss of control over their own inner reactions, unable to conquer their myriad fears and anxieties. This loss of control over both their inner and outer worlds commonly leads to a sense of helplessness and depression.

Barry, in his role as a firefighter, felt like a true macho guy—fit, strong, and fearless. He was well trained for emergencies, and routinely risked his life to protect others and save their homes. But when he couldn't save the woman who died in the fire, Barry's fundamental sense of power was shaken. His post-trauma beliefs included "I can't protect others," which motivated him to try to increase his control over various aspects of his life. He stayed vigilant when he left the house, reread all of his training manuals to determine how he had failed in his duty, and insisted that his family follow a strict schedule for outings.

Ian struggled to gain control over himself. He felt he had no power over his anxiety; at times, he felt violent impulses when he was angry with people at work. He feared he might one day act out and hit someone.

Angela, too, struggled with pervasive feelings of helplessness over her world. Katrina had destroyed her home and her entire community, and had taken her mother's life. Sometimes, she just felt so helpless and overwhelmed that she felt like she shouldn't even try to put her life back together.

Here are some of Barry's, Ian's, and Angela's changed beliefs about control:

- I can't protect others.

- I have no power to affect things in my life.

- I can't control myself (my fear, violent impulses).

- There's no sense in trying—I am helpless.

- Only through constant vigilance can I control what happens.

Step 1: What Are Your Own Beliefs about Control and Power Since the Trauma?

Think about and write down in your journal some of your own changed beliefs about power.

Step 2: Challenge Your Beliefs about Control

The beliefs that Barry, Angela, and Ian developed after their traumas are very common, and you probably identify with at least some of them. Notice that many of these beliefs assume they have *no* control or power—they are black or white statements.

Are your beliefs extreme in this way? We all need a sense of personal power in our lives, but it is true that there are many things that are outside of our control—hurricanes, earthquakes, fire, war, the actions of other people. This doesn't mean that we have no control, but it does mean that some things we have control over, others we don't.

> The serenity prayer adopted by Alcoholics Anonymous is a wise principle to live by, whether you believe in a Higher Power or not:
>
> *God grant me the serenity to accept the things I cannot change; courage to change the things I can; and wisdom to know the difference.*

Personal power relates to those aspects of your own behavior and life that you truly have control over. This may include where you work, your relationships, how you respond to conflicts, whether you chose a movie or to go for a walk. You even have the power to determine how you cope with your PTSD, which is why you are working through the chapters in this book. So while trauma underscores those aspects of life that are random or outside of our power to stop, it should not negate the power we have to make choices in our own lives.

Here's how to challenge your control beliefs:

- Consider whether your beliefs about control seem like all-or-nothing beliefs.

- If your beliefs do seem extreme ("I have no control"), can you come up with examples that don't fit your belief? Focus on aspects of yourself that you have power over.

- Think about other evidence that suggests your belief may be extreme and not realistic.

Step 3: Consider What May Be True about Your Beliefs

Angela's, Ian's, and Barry's post-trauma beliefs do contain a grain of truth: There are harmful events that cannot be stopped. Barry must realize that this is true no matter how thoroughly he reviews what happened, how well he prepares in the future, and how alert he remains throughout his life. He cannot control what is outside of his own behavior: Fires sometimes get out of control and kill people before they can be contained. Angela must also find a way to recognize that while she cannot stop hurricanes, she does have control over rebuilding her life.

Step 4: Revise Your Beliefs Regarding Control

What aspects of your life do you have power over, and what is beyond your control? It's important to acknowledge that there is only so much you can do to protect yourself or others. Your revised beliefs might therefore be that you can't completely eliminate the possibility of being the victim of a fire, tornado, abuse, assault, car accident, or some other trauma, but that you do have control over how you cope with it.

For example, "I have the power over the choices I make in my life, but I can't control what others do or larger events (accidents, acts of nature)."

Working through Changes in Beliefs about Yourself

After a trauma, many people notice a change in how they view themselves. It's a change in your core beliefs about who you are, your strengths and talents, your weaknesses, what you like and dislike, how you relate to others, and all your many personality traits.

These self-beliefs are how you define yourself, and include judgments about yourself as a human being. They are what determine your self-esteem and whether you think you are basically a good person, worthy of love and respect. Common changes in the self-beliefs of people with PTSD include believing that you are weak, damaged, worthless, or bad.

Because Ian froze during his assault, afterwards he believed he was incompetent and weak. He thought that a person who was confident and knew how to handle things would have fought back. Dan also believed that if he had been a better soldier, he could have saved Cesar. This is a common theme in trauma, that one could have acted differently and possibly stopped the trauma from occurring. Also, the fact that both Dan and Ian found themselves struggling to manage their anxiety, avoidance, and insomnia after their traumas further undermined any sense they had of inner strength or courage. Indeed, many people with PTSD feel that their symptoms indicate personal weakness.

Trauma survivors also struggle with a sense that they are damaged. They may view their PTSD symptoms as proof that their brains are broken, their minds shattered. Those of you who have sustained physical wounds from combat or a disaster or accident may be unable to carry out activities you once did with ease. Sonya's car accident left her with significant nerve damage to her left arm, so she could no longer work quickly on a computer or do anything that required two hands. She was on disability for months as she tried to learn how to use her right hand to do tasks, and she struggled with feeling useless.

Survivor's guilt and feeling unworthy of living are common responses for people who survived traumas in which others died or were injured. Angela was tortured by the idea that she might have saved her mother "if only" she had never put her in a retirement home, or had visited her that day, or had moved her before the hurricane came in. She felt responsible, and could not imagine trying to rebuild her life when her mother hadn't survived. Dan not only blamed himself for Cesar's death, he didn't understand why he was spared when other soldiers were killed. It didn't seem fair that he could sleep in his bed at night, hug his kids, and pursue his life when Cesar and other fallen soldiers in Iraq couldn't. Because Dan felt he was no more worthy than they were, he felt guilty about surviving.

Child abuse goes much deeper than simply changing one's self-beliefs. Because child abuse happens while a person's self-concept is still developing, it is often integrated into one's identity. When Nicole was being sexually abused by her uncle, she had no understanding of how an adult could inflict such a terrifying and awful act on a child. She turned her fear and shame inward into a belief that she was somehow responsible and different from other children, deserving of the abuse.

Many abuse survivors feel that they are *bad* in some fundamental way—if they weren't, they reason, the abuse would not have happened. Or they may feel that because of the abuse, they are forever tainted and unlovable. When any trauma happens in childhood—including not only abuse but the unexpected death of a family member or surviving a dangerous event—the resulting beliefs about the self require more work to challenge and change.

Here is a summary of some of the self-beliefs that can emerge following a trauma:

- "I am weak" (because I didn't fight back, can't control my symptoms).

- "I am damaged" (physically, emotionally).

- "I am useless" (because I cannot work or take care of tasks at home).

- "I am unworthy" (didn't deserve to survive the disaster).

- "I am guilty/shameful" (responsible for my abuse, letting others die, killing others in war).

Step 1: What Are Your Beliefs about Yourself Since the Trauma?

List these beliefs in your journal.

Step 2: Challenge Your Self-Beliefs

Trauma often causes people to draw overly harsh conclusions about themselves. Because humans try very hard to make sense of traumatic events, it's difficult to believe that bad things happen to good people. It's much easier to blame yourself and think that the trauma occurred because of your incompetence or bad character: "If only I were smarter/stronger/worthier/more moral, this would not have happened."

These beliefs that emerge about yourself after a trauma are very critical, very black or white. Take Ian, for example. Freezing is a natural response to terror, and not fighting back may actually have saved his life by not provoking his assailants. He should also remember that he was not the cause of the mugging—the criminals were. The same is obviously true for Nicole regarding her childhood abuse. As an adult, Nicole must work to change the shameful self-view that formed when she was a girl, and to recognize that her uncle was responsible for doing something an adult should never do to a child, no matter what the child says or does. And although

Angela may feel partly responsible for her mother's death, it was actually caused by a Category 5 hurricane in which thousands of others died. There was nothing that Angela, alone, could have done in the face of so massive a catastrophe.

Another error that trauma survivors make in judging themselves is to conclude something about their own character based on one situation or event. Ian may have frozen in a life-threatening situation, but that doesn't mean he can't handle emergencies. Dan may not have been able to save Cesar, but that does not mean he's incompetent or that he didn't save other lives. Nicole may have been victimized, but that does not make her a victim by nature. Drawing an extreme conclusion based on one fact or action is a particular type of black or white thinking. But how you acted during the trauma is only one example of your behavior, and everyone should get some slack for what they do under extraordinary, life-threatening circumstances.

See if you can challenge the beliefs you developed about yourself after the trauma:

- Are your beliefs about yourself extreme, black or white, harsh, or judgmental?

- Are you concluding something about your character based on one example of your behavior—how you acted during the trauma?

- If someone else did what you did during and after the trauma, what would you say about him or her?

- If your beliefs do seem extreme, can you come up with examples or evidence that don't fit your belief?

Step 3: Consider What May Be True about Your Belief (and What's Not)

Is there some piece of your belief that may be true? While concluding something about your character based on how you acted during and after the trauma is not really fair or realistic, it may be that you genuinely regret what you did.

This leads us to an important distinction between guilt and shame. If you do something that you regret or make a mistake but still feel you are a good person, you will feel guilty for the behavior. Guilt is a healthy emotion: You recognize that you did something you wish you hadn't, and you are motivated to acknowledge it and, if possible, make amends and apologize. But if you do something (or something happens to you) and believe it means that you are a bad person, you will feel shame. Shame is related to your core beliefs about who you are. When trauma cuts deeply into your sense of self-worth and goodness, you will experience shame, which is not a healthy emotion. Shame is related to making harsh and sweeping judgments about your nature based on the way you behaved during the trauma—it is the black or white error we described earlier.

If you regret a behavior, it is appropriate to feel guilt and find a way to rectify the situation, if possible. But if you feel shame, believing your behavior reflects something fundamentally bad or flawed about you, then you should challenge this judgment. For example, Angela regrets not moving her mother out of the nursing home when she first heard about the approaching hurricane. There are many reasons she didn't think she needed to, yet still she feels guilty. As long as she can keep from making a sweeping indictment of herself as a bad or incompetent daughter, she can work to accept her actions in the situation, and forgive herself.

Step 4: Revise and Accept Beliefs Regarding the Self

Now that you have examined your beliefs about yourself after the trauma, it is time to revise them. You can acknowledge making mistakes or struggling with your symptoms, but resist critical, sweeping self-judgments. Instead, acknowledge behaviors that show the opposite traits—your strengths, your courage, your positive efforts. Revise your self-beliefs to be balanced, fair, and forgiving.

For example, "I did not save Caesar, but I was able to protect other soldiers and am fighting hard to overcome my PTSD."

Working through Beliefs about Your Relationships

Trauma can profoundly affect your relationships, since others may not be able to understand what you are going through. Barry had difficulty relating to his fellow firefighters after his traumatic experience. They still acted as though they were immune to being hurt on the job; their daily bravado and casual attitude about fighting fires annoyed Barry, who knew firsthand that death could easily be part of their work. Because of his experience and PTSD, he also felt alienated from his wife and kids. How could they know what it was like to fail to save someone's life? While he was struggling with this debilitating guilt, anxiety, and depression, they were still shopping, watching sitcoms, and acting as if nothing had changed. Barry's beliefs about relationships had shifted: He was no longer certain that "normal" life with them had meaning. This is partly why he withdrew and had trouble being warm and affectionate.

Dan's daily life-and-death experiences with his fellow soldiers in Iraq also had a deep impact on his beliefs about the meaning of closeness. Within his unit, the soldiers developed an intense loyalty and commitment to one another, born out of their mutual courage and willingness to die for each other and their country. After Dan returned home, though, his relationships with friends and family felt trivial in comparison.

In traumas involving a death, there can be the added fear that relationships can involve loss and grief, which we'll talk about in chapter 13.

Relationship beliefs are particularly affected by a trauma that is caused by another person. If you have experienced sexual or physical abuse, assault, combat, or torture, your ability to trust other people may have been damaged—and that's understandable. Trauma can lead you to believe that people are capable of cruelty and aggression. Dan experienced firsthand what it was like to be shot at in Iraq, and learned that he was capable of killing another human being. Nicole's experience with abuse left her feeling betrayed, vulnerable, and unsafe in relationships. She would ask: If your trust has been violated once, why can't it happen again? There is, of course, some degree of truth to these thoughts. There are people who are capable of hurting you, but not all people are dangerous. The problem is, if you believe you should not trust other people, you won't open yourself up to intimacy and closeness.

Indeed, trauma usually leads people to withdraw from their relationships out of alienation, mistrust, and fear of loss, which are enhanced if you are also struggling with negative feelings about yourself, as we've talked about above. You may feel that the safest and easiest way to cope is to wall yourself off.

Here are some of Barry's, Dan's, and Nicole's beliefs about relationships that changed with their traumas:

- You can't trust anyone, not even your spouse or family.

- No one understands me anymore.

- I don't know how to be close to my friends and family anymore.

- People are violent and hurt each other.

- My family and friends are concerned with trivial things when people are dying.

- Unless someone has saved your life, you don't have a true bond.

- It's not safe to get close to people.

Step 1: What Are Your Beliefs about Others/Relationships Since the Trauma?

List them in your journal.

Step 2: Challenge Your Relationship Beliefs

While keeping your distance from others may seem like a natural response to these beliefs, there are two reasons why it actually leaves you more—not less—vulnerable. The first is that social support is one of the most important needs we have as human beings. It's been scientifically linked to emotional well-being and physical health, and it's essential for healing from PTSD. The second is that social withdrawal reinforces your belief that other people are not safe to get close to, and that you must stay on guard with others.

It's important to consider and challenge these beliefs. If one of your beliefs involves feeling different or estranged from others in your life since the trauma, this is not surprising. But do you believe that this will change over time? If your belief is hopeless ("No one understands me and they never will," or "I'll never be ever to love again"), remember that healing and recovery happen with time. You may be having trouble connecting right now, but as you heal and reach out (see chapter 8), you will rediscover how to be close again. And as you begin to talk about your experience with loved ones (see chapter 12), you will feel more understood by others. Try to revise your beliefs in a way that leaves open the possibility of recreating intimacy in your relationships.

Also consider whether your beliefs involve taking one experience (the trauma) and drawing a broad, black-or-white conclusion about all people that is increasing your mistrust. Just because Nicole's uncle was capable of sexual abuse doesn't mean all men act with aggression and with the intent to violate. The violence Dan experienced in Iraq is not the norm; it occurs mostly in situations of war or political repression—not anywhere or at any time.

To challenge your relationships beliefs:

- Review your beliefs to see if they are extreme and overly self-protective.

- If your beliefs do seem extreme, can you come up with examples that don't fit your belief?

- Challenge your belief that your estrangement from others will be forever.

- If, based on your trauma experience, you believe that people in general cannot be trusted, challenge this broad conclusion.

Step 3: Consider What May Be True about Your Belief

What is true about your relationship beliefs is that you probably *are* disconnected from friends and family to some extent right now.

And if you had an experience in which someone tried to hurt, violate, or kill you, your beliefs around trust should recognize that there are people out there who can't be trusted—but that doesn't mean everyone!

Step 4: Revise and Accept Beliefs Regarding Relationships

Now that you have examined your beliefs for potential errors as well as for what may be true, it is time to try to revise your core relationship beliefs. For example, you might want to consider the following belief: "I feel estranged from those I love right now, but I will be able to connect with them in time." Or if your beliefs involve mistrust: "It's been hard for me trust others since the trauma, but someday I'll be ready to open up to people who care about me." These statements acknowledge how you are feeling now, but also include a recognition that you want to change your relationships and not draw generalities from your traumatic experience.

Working through Purpose, Faith, and World Beliefs

In the broadest sense, trauma may have changed how you feel about the world and what is meaningful in your life. What used to be important—getting ahead at work, taking care of your kids, making improvements on your home, hanging out with friends—may now feel empty. A life-threatening experience can turn what felt normal in your life upside down, and cause you to lose your purpose or your faith. The daily struggle with PTSD can also keep you from investing in the future.

After her accident, Sonya felt like the curtain had been pulled aside to reveal a frightening, painful, and meaningless world. She still took care of her son, Eric, and eventually was able to work, but she had lost any desire to focus on her career and had difficulty imagining, and therefore creating, a fulfilling life for herself and Eric.

Angela had similar feelings for years after Hurricane Katrina. After witnessing all the death and destruction in her community and all the lives that had been altered forever, she felt foolish about trying to put down new roots in Houston. Why invest? What was the point? Living a "happy" life felt false to her, and, in some way, dishonorable given the suffering of so many others.

Dan shared this reluctance to live his life when so many had died in Iraq. Life back home also felt trivial and boring compared to his military purpose and the day-to-day intensity of his mission.

Like these individuals, you may have lost your way. Your daily life may no longer feel like it has purpose. Your dreams might lack the meaning they used to hold. There can also be a shift in your sense of the world as a just place. Most people want to believe that if you try to do the right thing in life, good things will follow. Trauma may force you to question order and morality in the world. How do you make sense of horrible, random events that hurt people?

If you are religious, trauma can deeply shake your faith. Nicole abandoned her childhood belief in a just God as she grew into adulthood and attempted to make sense of her abuse. She felt God had failed to protect her. Barry found himself doubting his spiritual beliefs as well. He could not make sense of his pastor's words that the woman's death he couldn't prevent was God's will. Dan struggled with a different aspect of his faith. Because he had killed insurgents during fighting in Iraq, he was afraid that he had committed an unforgivable sin. It didn't matter to him that his actions occurred during war, or that the men he killed were shooting at him and his unit. He wondered if he could truly be forgiven.

Here are some examples of how world beliefs can change after a trauma:

- The world is a painful place that lacks meaning.

- There is no reason to invest in the future when bad things can happen at any moment.

- I don't feel I have a purpose in life anymore.

- The concerns of daily life seem trivial to me.

- The world is not a just or moral place.

- My Higher Power didn't protect me or others.

- God cannot forgive me for what I've done.

Step 1: How Have Your Beliefs about the World, Faith, and Your Life Purpose Changed Since the Trauma?

Write down your beliefs in your journal.

Step 2: Challenge Your World Beliefs

Beliefs that express a lack of meaning or purpose in the world, a bleak future, or struggles with one's Higher Power are common and understandable after trauma. But they tend to make the same error as relationship beliefs: They are broad, over-generalized conclusions about God or the world based on one or several traumatic events.

The key for challenging these beliefs is to think about them in a less sweeping, all-or-nothing way. Perhaps your belief can be revised to see the world as having both beauty and ugliness in it. Perhaps there *is* meaning, but you must develop a more complex and nuanced view of the universe or of God, a view that includes the joys and inevitable painful losses of relationships, and a recognition of inspirational acts of courage and generosity as well as acts of brutality. As you consider your beliefs that you listed above, balance them with examples in your life that are positive or meaningful. Remember the times that friends have helped you out, when you have taken care of others, or when your community came together to overcome a problem.

Use this procedure for challenging your beliefs about the world, faith, and your life purpose:

- Consider whether any of your beliefs listed in your journal are extreme or overly generalized statements.

- If your beliefs do seem extreme, can you come up with examples that don't fit your belief?

- Think about other evidence that suggests your belief may be extreme and not realistic, and be willing to intergrate positive examples into your worldview.

Step 3: Consider What May Be True about Your Belief

Because you have experienced a trauma, you have seen something terrifying, brutal, and painful. This is a reality, and cannot be denied. Your traumatic experience has to be reconciled with your other experiences in the world. The idea is not to deny what you have seen, but to put it into perspective—to integrate it into your life. It's a slow and complicated process, but it can begin here.

Step 4: Revise and Accept Beliefs Regarding the World, Faith and Your Life Purpose

Revising your beliefs about the world and your spirituality, then, requires accepting what happened to you during the trauma, and finding a way to balance it with the good experiences you have had of others and the world. You might also contemplate how you can create positive meaning from what happened to you: Perhaps you learned a valuable lesson from the trauma, or discovered aspects of your resiliency. You might also view the trauma as a challenge to help others and make the world a more compassionate place. A loss of morality or justice can be restored with new actions that have this intention. We'll talk much more about the process of restoring purpose and meaning after trauma in chapter 13.

Are there some positive meanings or lessons that your trauma has taught you? For instance, "While I have seen some awful things, I have a new purpose to work for justice and compassion in my relationships and work."

Moving Forward

It takes time, reflection, and work to figure out how your beliefs about yourself, safety, control, relationships, and life purpose have changed. It will be helpful to continue to write about these issues in the next chapter (journaling about the trauma), and to explore this with your therapist. You may also want to talk to close friends and family by using the techniques described in chapter 12. However you decide to continue this process of understanding and revising your deeply held beliefs, know that this is an important part of healing from a trauma.

CHAPTER 11

Processing the Trauma by Putting It into Words

Sonya

Sonya didn't talk about the car accident to anyone. She had nightmares about it several times a week, in which she would wake up shaking and drenched with perspiration. Images of the experience also popped into her mind at work and especially when she was around her son, Eric. She fought to keep these memories away, and found the idea of talking about the accident scary. But after her physical therapist referred her to a psychologist, Sonya slowly started to tell her therapist her story. While it did cause her anxiety, she found that putting the experience into words brought relief with time. She started having fewer nightmares and intrusive images, and thinking about the accident felt less terrifying. She also began to explore the meaning of the experience (how it changed her beliefs about herself and the world), and how she might use her trauma to change some of her life priorities.

■

Barry

Barry started writing about the fire around the one-year anniversary of the event. His psychiatrist had suggested it, and because Barry was someone who largely kept to himself and didn't want to upset his wife by talking to her about the experience, it was easier to put the trauma into words by journaling. At first, he felt pretty detached when he wrote about the fire. But as he was able to write about his unsuccessful attempt to save the woman's life, a rush of sadness and guilt broke through. Over the next month, Barry continued to write periodically, gradually focusing on how the trauma had challenged his belief that he was omnipotent and could protect everyone. And then he started writing about what his family meant to him.

Most people with PTSD avoid thinking and talking about their traumas. This avoidance is natural because of the intensely painful feelings associated with the trauma, including anxiety, grief, fear, guilt, and shame. You probably spend a lot of energy fighting the intrusive memories, avoiding reminders of the trauma, and trying to hold it together when you can't contain the flood of emotion. So why focus on the trauma when it brings up such painful feelings that threaten to overwhelm you? Because avoidance, in the long run, *maintains* the fear and the pain, and keeps you trapped by the memory.

While it is difficult to face your traumatic experience, putting it into words and exploring how deeply it has affected you are essential to healing. It's called working through the trauma, and there are several reasons it is so important.

The first is because therapy techniques that focus on telling the trauma story can effectively reduce the re-experiencing symptoms of PTSD, such as intrusive memories, images, nightmares, and flashbacks. This happens because confronting the memory over time in a safe environment reduces the anxiety associated with it. The act of putting the experience into words also reorganizes the memory in your brain, enabling you to finally put it into the past, where it belongs.

Another reason that trauma-focused work is important is that it helps you clarify the ways in which the traumatic experience may have challenged your beliefs (chapter 10), and how you might learn and grow from the experience (chapter 13).

Finally, working through the trauma with a therapist and learning how to talk about it with your close friends and family can help you feel more understood and connected to others. We'll talk about this process in chapter 12.

In this chapter, we describe how verbalizing the trauma transforms the memory. We also illustrate the kind of trauma-focused work you can do in therapy, and offer a set of structured exercises to help you process your traumatic experience using this book, through journaling about the event.

The timing of when you do this trauma-focused work is important. We saved these chapters on thinking, writing, and talking about the trauma for the end of the book because it is important that you first master the skills covered in section 2. Those skills will help you reduce your depression, manage your anxiety, and improve your social support systems before embarking on this next step of the recovery journey. You should also feel relatively stable in your symptoms and emotionally ready to do this work, and the best scenario is to have a therapist who can help you and provide support. Take a look at the box below to see when you *shouldn't* do this work.

Even if you decide you are not ready right now to work through the exercises, we encourage you to read through this chapter to learn about trauma memories and how to process them, so you have this important knowledge and skill for your PTSD toolbox.

When *Not* to Begin Processing the Trauma

We recommend that you do not do the journaling exercises in this chapter if you are experiencing any of the following:

- Severe depression or thoughts of hurting yourself or others.

- Overwhelming anxiety—you have not mastered skills in section 2.

- Excessive alcohol or drug use.

- Psychotic or severe dissociative symptoms.

- You are still in a potentially traumatic situation, such as an abusive relationship.

- You are having significant difficulty functioning at home, work, or school.

- You feel that you are not emotionally "ready" right now.

Why Putting the Trauma into Words Is Essential to Healing

To understand why talking about the trauma promotes recovery, you must understand how a trauma obstructs memory. In chapter 2, we explained how stressful situations trigger your alarm system. We described how trauma, as a severe and often life-threatening stressor, puts your alarm system into overdrive and floods your brain and body with adrenalin and cortisol. Your brain is designed to respond to elevated levels of these stress hormones, but when the levels get too high, an area of your brain responsible for forming memory gets overwhelmed. This brain region, called the hippocampus, normally processes an experience and organizes it into memory. Part of that processing is constructing a verbal story of what happened ("I went to work, checked email, then had lunch"). During a traumatic experience, however, the hippocampus is swamped with stress hormones and cannot do its job. The trauma memory is not processed coherently—it is dissociated into highly emotional and fragmented pieces. The memory of the trauma becomes disorganized, with images and thoughts that are intensely charged with fear, anger, guilt, and anguish.

This is why people with PTSD have intrusive images, thoughts, and nightmares: The trauma memory is like a bunch of loose, disconnected live wires in the brain—not a happy state for your mind! The reason you continue to have re-experiencing symptoms with PTSD is that your brain is still trying to organize the trauma experience, since it was unable to do so at the time. Your brain wants to work through the trauma, get some sense of resolution, and calm itself. The problem is, you automatically try to avoid anything that triggers the fear-infused memories. But it should be clear by now that avoidance only makes things worse. The more you try not to think about the trauma, the more the memories want to surface. You can't run from the memories, and you can't destroy them, either. Trying to suppress your thoughts and feelings ultimately only gives them more power—and you less control.

Directly facing your trauma is a necessary, but hard, step to take. You have to process the memory to put it into the past, and you have to understand and integrate how the experience has affected your life.

Putting the trauma into words does three things:

1. It organizes the trauma memory in the brain so that the re-experiencing symptoms go down.

2. It reduces the intensity and uncontrollability of the emotions associated with the memory.

3. It enables you to understand the trauma's impact on your core beliefs, and opens the way to growth.

When you start to talk or write about the trauma, you begin to put the pieces together and are able to experience the emotion without being quite so overwhelmed. As you verbalize what happened, you are literally connecting pathways that represent different aspects of the experience in your brain—visual memories, thoughts, sounds, feelings, physical sensations, and beliefs. Creating a narrative also helps you understand and process the fear, helplessness, guilt, and shame. It reduces the terror of the memory, and the intense emotions that feel so out of control slowly become more manageable as you make sense of the event. This doesn't mean that the painful feelings completely go away, just that you take ownership of them, learn to tolerate them, and ultimately develop a sense of acceptance for what happened.

As you tell your trauma story, you will begin to discover how your core beliefs about yourself, other people, and the world have changed. You may realize that you are going about your life as if an important part of yourself has been lost, or living as if the world or other people are not safe. There is meaning wrapped up with the trauma—beliefs that formed out of the trauma experience which we started to explore in chapter 10. While you may only partly be conscious of these post-trauma beliefs, they are nonetheless influencing your choices and behavior. Exploring these beliefs is an important part of processing the trauma. You may discover that your post-trauma views are distorted and overprotective, so that they are limiting your life and relationships. Processing the trauma should also increase your awareness and appreciation of your resiliency and the positive ways you coped in the situation and afterwards. By putting the trauma into a balanced, narrative form, you can start to draw on your knowledge and strengths in order to explore the meaning of what happened—and to begin healing.

When and How to Work through the Trauma

First, it is important to consider the timing of doing trauma-focused work. You should be aware that when you start working through your memories, it is likely that your anxiety and other symptoms will increase temporarily as you confront the trauma. Most people find this work a little scary, so we recommend that you *begin only after you feel fairly stable and have mastered the coping skills* from section 2. You need to feel ready before wading in. It's also helpful to have people in your life who can provide support.

You should not begin trauma-focused work if you are experiencing anything outlined in the box on page 230. This includes overwhelming anxiety, having thoughts of hurting yourself or others, having trouble functioning at home or work, experiencing psychotic symptoms, or using alcohol or drugs excessively. If you are still in an ongoing trauma situation (such as an abusive relationship), you will need to get out of that situation and get some breathing room before you begin processing the trauma.

The next issue is how to work through the trauma. We recommend that you have a three-pronged approach: Work with a therapist, write about the experience in a journal, and talk to friends and family. We will discuss processing the trauma through therapy and journaling in this chapter; the next chapter provides techniques for how to talk with the people in your life about the trauma, once you have done some of the trauma work on your own.

Working with a Therapist

The reason that therapy is so important when you first decide to work on the trauma is that for most people with PTSD, the trauma memory and associated feelings are intensely painful and difficult to confront. It helps to have someone trained in PTSD treatment who can listen to your trauma story and provide guidance and support. A psychotherapist can help you manage your feelings, safely explore the meaning of the event for you, and help you find positive ways to heal. If you are at all concerned about your ability to examine the trauma on your own, you should do this work within a therapeutic relationship. There are many different types of mental health professionals you can work with, including psychologists, psychiatrists, social workers, marriage and family therapists, and psychiatric nurses. The important thing in selecting a psychotherapist is that he or she should have specific training and experience in treating PTSD.

There are several specific approaches that use very structured techniques to help people process the trauma memory. One approach developed by Dr. Edna Foa is called Prolonged Exposure, and substantial research demonstrates that it is an effective treatment for PTSD. After a number of sessions where the therapist and individual with PTSD get acquainted and mutually plan the upcoming exposures, the therapist has the client describe the traumatic event (for example, a rape) in session from the beginning to end, as if it were happening right then ("I am walking outside my apartment, it's cold, my car is parked across the street . . .") for a minimum of 45 to 60 minutes. This memory exposure is repeated a number of times over subsequent sessions. Each exposure is audiotaped so the client can listen to the tapes between sessions. What happens over time is that the intensity of the anxiety and other emotions goes down with each retelling, and the trauma survivor learns that he or she will not lose control or be harmed by facing the trauma. The story also becomes more coherent and organized as the person naturally includes more detail, fills in gaps, and integrates different aspects of the experience.

Other approaches that focus on the trauma and have scientific evidence supporting their effectiveness include Cognitive Processing Therapy (CPT) and Eye Movement Desensitization and Reprocessing therapy (EMDR). CPT, developed by Patricia Resick, has the client write about the trauma experience and focus on how the trauma has affected his or her beliefs about self, others, and the world. What emerges in the writing is discussed and worked through with the therapist. In EMDR, the client thinks about the trauma experience while the therapist provides "bilateral stimulation." For example, the therapist moves her fingers back and forth across the client's right/left visual field and the client is instructed to follow them with his or her eyes—hence the "eye movement" in EMDR.

Journaling about the Trauma

The next sections of this chapter will describe how you can use journaling on your own to start processing the trauma. Journaling, like talking to someone, helps you to overcome the tendency to avoid the trauma memory so that you can work through the experience. Writing helps you put words to the trauma and organize it into a narrative. It allows you to explore the meaning of the event, and the different ways the experience has affected you.

In his research on writing about difficult or traumatic experiences, Dr. James Pennebaker found that people's essays, through repeated writing about the event, become more organized over time. Each time the story is retold, the writer starts making more causal links between events and feelings, and the narrative becomes clearer and more coherent. In other words, the act of writing helps the writer to make sense of what happened. He also found that writing for less than an hour several times over a week seemed to reduce the writers' vulnerability to illness—fewer visits to the doctor and quicker recovery from colds!

As you know, focusing on your trauma memory is difficult and will bring up strong emotions, particularly anxiety. This is the reason most people avoid the trauma memory. The advantage of writing is that you can control the timing and intensity of the memory exposure. You can write a little each day, or space it out over a week. You can decide when to stop. We do recommend, however, that when you sit down to write, you should try to write for a minimum of thirty minutes. The key (as in chapter 4 on avoidance) is always to stay with your anxiety long enough to experience it coming down—and it will. You do not want to start writing, become anxious, and then stop and escape; this will reinforce and increase your fear and avoidance. And like the exposure work in chapter 4, you will repeat the writing exercise a number of times.

While you can decide how frequently you want to write, we recommend that you try to write at least twice a week so that you are actively organizing the memory and working through the issues that come up. Again, it is helpful to be in therapy while processing traumatic memories so that, as you plunge into difficult material while journaling, you have a psychotherapist you can talk to as well. It is also helpful to have someone in your life who can provide support while you do this work.

Step 1: Prepare for Journaling by Reviewing Coping Skills

Before you begin writing, look again at the Anxiety Scale on page 47. You will be using this scale during your journaling. Next, review the anxiety management skills in chapter 3. We especially encourage you to use the following techniques:

- Skill 2: Alarm Sensations are Harmless
- Skill 3: Riding out the Anxiety
- Skill 4: Grounding Techniques
- Skill 5: Slow Breathing

Step 2: Determine the Time and Setting

Pick a place that is quiet and comfortable where you can write, and choose a time when you won't be interrupted or have to stop unexpectedly. You should write for 30 to 60 minutes. We encourage you to have a dedicated notebook for this process. You can use the journal you've already been writing in for this book. You may, however, want to have a separate notebook for writing about the trauma, which you can put away when you are done.

Step 3: Select Which Trauma to Write About

Your trauma may have been a single event, such as Ian's assault or Sonya's car accident. But if your trauma stretched out over days (as did Angela's experience with Katrina), months (Dan's combat exposure in Iraq), or included many instances (such as Nicole's abuse), then you need to decide what to write on. If you are working with a therapist, we recommend you start with the most intense or disturbing part of the trauma. If you are doing this on your own, you will need to use your judgment. Pick the part of the trauma (or a particular event) that really stands out in your memory and feels important. Then pick a start point (when you first became anxious during the actual event) and a finish point (when it felt like the event was essentially over or no longer threatening). After you have written about this event a number of times (see the steps below), you can do this procedure again with a different event.

Step 4: Describe the Trauma (First Time Telling of the Story)

You will be writing about your trauma memory a number of times. The first time, just try to describe what happened from start to finish, and focus on what you perceived through your senses—what you saw, heard, smelled, felt. As you tell the story, also include any thoughts and feelings you had during the experience. It is likely that there will be things you can't remember. Don't worry about that, and don't try to "recover" any memories. There will also be moments that are particularly difficult to write about. Just do your best to move through the experience.

Write continuously about what happened, from your start point until your designated end point for your event. Go for at least 30 minutes (up to one hour), and see if you can complete the description in that time. If you can't finish within the hour, just stop where you are when the time is up. You can finish the story the next time you write, preferably in a day or two—don't wait longer than a week.

As you write, it is important that you activate a certain level of anxiety; if you don't, you probably aren't accessing the emotional part of the memory. You will also want to control how high your anxiety gets. To track your anxiety, rate it on the 1 to 10 anxiety scale (page 47) every five minutes or so, and also when you hit sections of the memory that are very intense. Write your anxiety ratings in the margin of your paper. If your emotion rises above 8, you might stop for a minute and do some deep breathing or grounding. Once you're calmer, be sure to continue, and remember to tell yourself that your memory and the anxiety associated with it are not dangerous. If you are having little emotional reaction to the writing, you might try writing in present tense ("I am walking toward my car . . .") to get more engaged in the memory.

After you complete your journaling for the day, you should reward your courage and hard work by doing something that is soothing or pleasurable: taking a long bath, watching your favorite movie or show, taking a walk in a beautiful place, having a special meal. You decide how you will treat yourself, and write down what you rewarded yourself with at the end of your journaling for this day.

Step 5: Retell the Story

It is not enough to write out your story once; you need to process your memory and organize it over time for the intense emotion to come down. Wait at least one or two days, then set aside time to write in your journal. This time, allow 30 to 60 minutes to describe again what happened, from start to finish, and include any thoughts and feelings you had during the experience. You may find that you start to fill in more details, but don't try too hard: What you remember will naturally emerge over time, and it is normal to forget some pieces of the memory. Every five minutes, rate your emotion on the anxiety scale and write it on the margin of your journal. Also record your score whenever your emotions are strong.

Sometimes during the most intense moments of a trauma, you may feel yourself detach or go numb. At the time, this was a way of avoiding what was overwhelming. Now, see if you can stay focused on what you are seeing and feeling in those moments. If your anxiety gets very high (an 8 or higher), take a one-minute break, breathe, ground yourself, and then continue. When you are finished, reward yourself again for your strength and perseverance, and write down what the reward is in your journal.

Step 6: Repeat the Story and Focus on Your Beliefs

Repetition is the key to overcoming anxiety and working through the memory. Now that you've told your trauma story twice, you should repeat the procedure several more times, this time focusing on how the trauma altered some of your core beliefs about safety, control, relationships, identity, and meaning in the world. These were the topics of chapter 10, so you might want to review them before beginning this step.

Much of what is important about PTSD has to do with the *meaning* of the experience to you. Write about how the trauma may have undermined your feelings of safety in the world, trust in other people, your life purpose or your sense of self. Explore how your beliefs about justice, faith, and the world may have been challenged by your experience.

Step 7: Closure

While it is possible to write endlessly about your trauma, there is a time to stop. The goal of this chapter is to reduce your anxiety associated with your trauma memory and to increase your understanding and acceptance of the experience. There will be a natural stopping point to this process, and it is important to determine when that is and to wrap up your trauma journaling.

This is the guideline: If your anxiety never gets above a 3 on the anxiety scale during your journaling, and if you can write your trauma narrative in a clear, organized, and coherent way, you've reached the stopping point. If you find that you've written about the same trauma event repeatedly (more than a dozen times) and your anxiety has not come down significantly, we recommend that you stop. While talking and writing about the trauma is effective for most people, it may not be helping you. If you are in therapy, you can talk to your mental health provider about it.

If your trauma included a series of events that continue to haunt you in nightmares and intrusive thoughts, you should go through steps 1 through 7 with another event. For example, Angela might write first about the most intense moment during Katrina, such as when the hurricane winds reached their peak and news reports indicated that the hurricane was a category 5. After working through the steps with this event, Angela might then pick another frightening moment (when the water levels started rising in her house) to process. Dan could chose three of the most life-threatening or disturbing experiences in Iraq to write about separately. We suggest you consider stopping at three events, and give yourself several months to see how you feel after processing these memories. If at a later date there are still several trauma memories you want to work through, you can journal about those.

When you are finished, you should create a simple ritual to mark the end of this very courageous work, perhaps placing all the pages with your trauma story in a book and putting it away in a special place. Then, do something extra special for yourself on this day—acknowledge your strength, celebrate your resiliency, and reward yourself!

Moving Forward

Once you have worked through your trauma experience through journaling and/or therapy, consider sharing it with someone you feel safe with and close to. Talking to your friends or family will help you feel less alone, and can increase their support and empathy. But you need to know *how* to talk to them about the trauma in a way that is comfortable for you and them. The next chapter provides you—and your trusted confidants—the tools to do this.

CHAPTER 12

How to Talk about Trauma and PTSD with Others

Dan

After Dan started therapy at the Veterans Administration and began to work through the fear and guilt associated with his combat experience in Iraq, he noticed that his chronic anxiety started to go down. He could still be triggered by reminders of combat (hot days, sudden loud noises, the smell of smoke), but he found he could de-escalate the anxiety with slow breathing and grounding—he especially liked to recite lyrics from Green Day songs as a way to distract himself. He had stopped drinking and using marijuana, and his wife, Heather, had moved back in with him. Dan was clearly on the road to recovery, but he still felt distant from Heather. She tiptoed around him, and they sat at the dinner table in silence. He missed his Army buddies, and felt alone in his own home even when his family was around. When he went out with friends, no one talked about the war; when, on a rare occasion, someone would ask about his experience in Iraq, he didn't know how to respond. He would clench his jaw and say something vague like "It was ugly." Everywhere he went, he was like a ghost. He knew he needed to find a way to reconnect to his hometown, his friends, and his family, but he didn't know how.

Nicole

Nicole was also making progress with her therapist. She was talking about the sexual abuse for the first time, and starting to see that many of her fears as an adult had links back to when she was seven years old, when her uncle had started touching her. She could see more clearly why she had so much discomfort with sex—and even physical affection—and how it was straining her relationship with her fiancé, Peter. During the abuse, Nicole had retreated within her protective walls and kept her vulnerable side hidden. In high school she had put up a tough front for others. She grew into a woman who got things done and didn't tolerate excuses or "mushy" emotion. She thought of herself as confident, cool-headed, practical, and highly successful competing in sales, but others found her rigid and cold. Peter was her first relationship that had lasted longer than a few months, and for the first time she found herself wanting to let down her guard with him. But as she did, a flurry of anxiety and anger erupted inside her. Nicole and Peter were fighting more, and what little physical intimacy they had was disappearing. She knew she needed to talk to him more about her past, but the idea terrified her, and she didn't know where to begin.

Many people with PTSD struggle with feeling alone and alienated from others. They emerge from a disaster, childhood abuse, car accident, assault, or war and no longer know how to talk to their friends and family. For you, the trauma survivor, the world has changed, but others are still living their normal lives—going to work, planning meals, rooting for their favorite team on television. "Normal" for them may feel strange or meaningless to you now. A giant gap has formed between you and those you once felt close to. You feel different. No one understands what you've been through, or what it is like to be living in your skin.

What is needed is a way to start bridging that gap. This chapter is about doing just that—learning how you can start sharing some of your experience with those you are close to so that you feel less alone and more connected. At the end of the chapter, we also give suggestions for the listener, which you can show to your friend or family member.

Talking to a Therapist is Different from Talking to Family and Friends

In the previous chapter, we addressed the importance of working through the trauma with a professional therapist and on your own through writing. Once you start putting the trauma into words, you learn that you can tolerate the memory and feelings associated with it. Over time, the traumatic memory becomes more organized and manageable—a story about something you experienced in the past, rather than an event that lives on and causes you overwhelming fear or shame.

Dan and Nicole both emerged from their psychotherapy and journal writing with a better understanding of their feelings and beliefs about the traumatic events. After this work, they experienced fewer nightmares and intrusive memories. They had turned trauma into narrative, and while this would never take away the painful memories, they had developed a crucial awareness, acceptance, and control over those memories.

If you have been working through your trauma experience and know that you can talk about it without feeling overwhelmed, you may wonder whether you should share any of the experience with your spouse, family, or friends. One of the ways trauma can be so damaging is that it can lead to a sense of alienation. Though you may want your loved ones to know what happened, you hesitate. You're not sure whether to talk about "it." You may be like many traumatized people who never want to talk about their trauma experience for fear that others won't be interested, won't understand, or will become upset hearing the story. You may think you should protect your family and friends from what you have experienced. So what do you do? Most choose to keep silent.

There is a better way. You can talk about "it," but the key is to learn how. You may be surprised to learn that the most beneficial part of talking about a traumatic experience *is not to recount the details of the trauma itself, but to share how the trauma has affected you.* The way you talk to mental health professionals about PTSD or write about it in your journal (which involves going into specifics about the trauma) is different from the way you should talk to your spouse and others you are close to. This chapter will teach you the skills to communicate your trauma experience in a way that is healthy, safe, and empowering for both you and your loved ones. The idea is to reconnect in a meaningful way and to gain the social support you need to continue with your recovery.

Why Talking about It Can Be Helpful

Trauma has a deep and transforming effect on the survivor. At first, you may feel shattered by the experience. Later, you struggle with debilitating fear and other symptoms that have been described. The experience likely changed how you work, how you relate to others, and how you move through the world. It may have altered your sense of safety and control, your values and beliefs, your spirituality. How do you *not* talk with your loved ones about something that has affected you so deeply?

Take a second to think about what makes you feel close to your family or friends. To a large extent, it is probably feeling understood by them. They have a sense of your strengths (your great sense of humor, your street smarts, your compassion, how you stay cool under pressure), and what you don't like (spiders, spinach, and going on long flights). They recognize your talents (you can fix anything, bake the best desserts, play a mean game of basketball), and know your values (parenting first, working for the environment, duty to serve your country). You can be open and honest with them. They "get you." Because of this, when you spend time together, the interaction feels genuine, and you know that you can talk about what's real, what matters.

But trauma can change this. People with PTSD often resist talking about it even with their closest friends, partners, or family members for many reasons. You may fear that if you talk about your experience, it will be upsetting to you or the other person. You may be afraid that others will criticize or think less of you for what you did or didn't do. Or you may not want to talk about having PTSD because you are afraid others will think that you are weak, damaged, or crazy. Maybe you did try to talk about your experience, but the other person didn't respond the way you wanted him to. All of these concerns are quite common. Some of them explain why people with PTSD feel more comfortable talking to others who have been through a similar traumatic experience.

For these reasons, you may be reluctant to share what you are
going through with family and friends. Yet consider what happens
when you keep silent. Trauma becomes the elephant in the room
that no one dares to talk about. Your life and your relationships
have been altered, yet you say nothing, your friends say nothing,
your spouse says nothing. And so now the conversation feels false
and superficial. You go through the motions of making dinner or
going to a movie, but your internal reality has nothing to do with
what is happening on the outside. While you may be working on
your trauma in therapy, with everyone else you are struggling alone,
which is a very hard and lonely place.

Why then is it important to start sharing some of your experience with those you are close to? One very important reason is
because silence keeps you alone. The act of opening up and sharing
something that has such a profound impact on your life is an act of
trust that will bring you closer to the other person. There is now
plenty of scientific research that confirms how harmful it can be to
keep things private—and how beneficial it can be to talk.

It isn't necessary that your family and close friends know
exactly what occurred during the traumatic experience. What is

essential is that they know you trust them and are willing to let them in. And it is important that you come to realize that they care. As long as they try to understand, you will no longer feel so separated from them. Notice we said *try*. When you see that they are attempting to listen compassionately and that they want to understand, you'll feel better. Your talking will help them to provide the right kind of support when you need it. In addition, because trauma does affect your relationships, talking about it can also be a relief to your family and friends. By talking, you've given the elephant a way to gracefully leave the room.

If Dan can find a way to talk with Heather, then later when his anxiety rockets through the roof while hearing a news report about Iraq, he doesn't need to hide it from her. He will simply look at her as his heart starts racing, and she will nod, knowing from earlier conversations what it means to him to see those images. And if Nicole can talk to Peter about how her abuse has affected her, when she freezes in response to his affectionate touch, they can talk about it instead of blaming each other.

Who Do You Talk To?

The most important thing in selecting someone to confide in about your experience recovering from trauma is trust. Is the individual someone who you can usually be open with, and who will be empathetic and supportive? Sometimes the answer will be obvious: It may be your spouse, boyfriend or girlfriend whom you share everything with, a sister or brother, or a friend who is your primary confidant. But if you are not sure about how someone might respond (i.e., he or she might become upset or critical), it's important to think carefully about whether to share. The level of intimacy in your relationship is a factor. It is more important to consider letting in your spouse than a friend at work. And even if right now you don't feel so connected to your spouse, if you felt close before the trauma, he or she is probably someone who is safe to talk to—and talking will help restore some of your intimacy.

If you have one or more individuals in mind, but are afraid of how they may respond (or if earlier attempts to talk to them have not gone well), you might direct them to the last section of this chapter for family and friends. No matter who you talk to, you should always first ask the individual about whether he or she would be comfortable with you sharing some of your experience. After you have completed this chapter, you can tell those who you plan to talk to what to expect from the conversation, reassuring them that it will not include any gory details of the trauma. Then you can say what you would like from them, which is simply to try to understand and not give advice.

What's Important to Share?

You may think that the most important part of talking about trauma is telling the details of the traumatic experience. While this is a central component of certain treatments for PTSD (such as exposure therapy and journaling about the trauma), it isn't necessary in order for you to feel more connected and supported.

As we described in the previous chapter, much of what is significant about the experience of going through a trauma—and what you should focus on when sharing—is how the experience has affected you. This includes how you feel about yourself, whether the trauma has challenged your beliefs about the world or your spirituality, what symptoms you've been struggling with, and how you have been drawing on your strengths to overcome PTSD.

Structuring the Conversation

The following sections will describe what to talk about and what not to talk about. We will also provide examples and talking points, which will model exactly how you can share your experience with your family and close friends.

Leave Out the Trauma Details

Again, this may seem strange at first, but you really don't need to talk much about the trauma itself. Think about the goals of the conversation. In therapy, an essential goal is to process the trauma itself, to confront the vulnerable, painful feelings around the event, and to work through the meaning of the event for you. Your goal in talking to close family or friends is different: It is to feel less alone and more connected. They don't need to know more than a general outline of the event to support you in this way, and it is likely they know basically what happened.

But if they don't, here are several examples of how much to say about the trauma:

- Nicole: "When I was in elementary school, I was molested by my uncle."

- Dan: "When I was in Iraq, I saw a lot of combat. I lost several buddies including my close friend Cesar."

- Angela: "I lived in New Orleans when Hurricane Katrina hit. My mother died in the storm and I lost my house."

You don't need to say any more than that. You can even keep it more general: "I am an abuse survivor," "I was a combat soldier in Iraq."

We encourage you not to focus on the event itself because it can be emotionally risky for you and the listener, and, as you will learn in this chapter, there is much about your experience that is important and valuable to discuss that isn't about the trauma details. If your listener asks questions about the event that start to take you into painful specifics of the trauma, you should check your level of comfort. You may have a relationship with a close family member or friend in which you know you can safely talk about what happened. But if you have any misgivings about going more deeply into the event, you can say:

- "Rather than focus on the [abuse, war, mugging, hurricane, accident], I'd like to try to tell you what it's meant to me."

- "What would be really helpful is to tell you about what it's been like since then—living with PTSD, trying to conquer it."

- "What I'd like to tell you about is how deeply it affected me, and how I've been working to overcome the experience."

Thank them for their interest. They aren't trying to be intrusive, though it may sometimes feel that way.

Talk about Your PTSD

One of the most important things to share is how you have been struggling with PTSD. The symptoms of PTSD have had a profound affect on your life. Tell the listener about your reactions—the nightmares, difficulty sleeping, irritability, unexpected triggers that set off anxiety, avoiding situations and places that make you anxious, withdrawing, or getting angry at others. Tell them how these symptoms interfere with your school, work, relationships, and daily life. Maybe you had to stop working, separated from your partner, or did poorly at school. Share this with your spouse, friend, or family member. Describe both the problems you had after the trauma and the ones you are still struggling with.

Dan might talk about his sense of alienation when he returned, how he started drinking to get some relief from his anxiety and guilt, and his angry outbursts at home. He can talk about how he continues to feel irritable a lot of time, and still sometimes avoids crowds and driving, which limits what he can do. Nicole may describe how she hardened as an adult, how she has resisted closeness even in her friendships, and that she still has difficulties with physical intimacy in relationships. Whatever aspects of PTSD you have struggled with, share them with those you are close to. You can also ask them to read chapter 2 so they can understand the nature of PTSD, chapters 9 through 11 on relationship issues, and the last section of this chapter.

Share How Your Identity, Purpose, and Beliefs Have Changed

Trauma is so different from other experiences because it challenges your core sense of self, safety, control, and meaning in the world. The safe and predictable world of Nicole's childhood was ripped away by two years of fear and violation. For years, she felt dirty and damaged, but she responded to her shame by acting as a confident, accomplished, no-nonsense force to be reckoned with. In Iraq, Dan had many near misses and came close to losing his life; he continues to be haunted by the fact that he couldn't save his buddy. These experiences left him with the sense that he has very little control in his world, and that no one is immune to sudden death. Nicole and Dan were transformed by the traumas.

What is important about trauma is not usually the event itself, but what happened to you as a consequence: how it changed the way you see yourself, how it affected the way you relate to others, how it altered your beliefs about the world. This is what you can share about the trauma—*what it means to you, how it has changed you.* Draw on what you've clarified through the exercises in chapter 10 on how the trauma challenged your beliefs, as well as the final chapter in this book, which focuses on how people grow from the experience, rediscover their faith, and become closer to those they love. You should share both the good and bad that have come from trauma, and where you are in the process of overcoming your PTSD.

Dan started talking to Heather after joining a support group for Iraq and Afghanistan vets at the VA. At first, he just wanted her to get a sense of how things were over there. He described what the days were like, the types of duties they had, what missions were most dangerous. This enabled Heather to get a feel for what it was like. Later, after his individual psychotherapy helped him to feel less agitated and avoidant about his most traumatic experience in Iraq—the explosion that killed Cesar—Dan was able to share with Heather the impact that had on him. He knew not to go into any gory details about it, but there was something he did want her to know:

DAN: *The hardest part about what happened with Cesar is the feeling that I should have known. We'd been on that road before, and it was always rigged. I remember having a weird feeling before it happened. I saw a wrecked car parked off in the distance, in middle of nowhere, and felt the hair in my neck rise. I should have shouted for us to halt, but I didn't. I just keep feeling I could have stopped it from happening.*

I live with this guilt every day. I also wonder why it wasn't me who was killed.

For Dan there is grief about losing his friend, but there is also guilt and a sense of powerlessness. Even though there was probably nothing he could have done, many vets feel responsible for the deaths of their fellow soldiers. This is also common for police, emergency responders, firefighters, and disaster workers. For Dan, the experience also made him wonder why Cesar was killed and not him—how could death be so random or arbitrary? The trauma challenged his sense of morality in the world. What Dan has done here that is so important is that he let Heather see that he is struggling with guilt, and with the meaning of Cesar's death. Heather's job is not to take that guilt or pain away, but just to try to understand Dan's torment.

Nicole began to realize through her therapy just how much her experience of being molested had affected her romantic relationships. Over time, she began to share some of this with Peter:

NICOLE: *After being molested, I cringed when people touched me. I didn't like my parents hugging me. I dated, but I really struggled with the physical affection, and often I would end up breaking up with the guy. Peter, I want to be able to hold hands with you, to be affectionate, to be sexually intimate. But it is really hard for me. I get scared. I don't feel safe.*

Before Nicole starting talking to Peter about this, she reacted out of fear and anger whenever he reached for her hand or snuggled in bed. She accused him of being insensitive and aggressive, and she felt ashamed. The power of talking about how a trauma has affected you is that it brings closeness and understanding rather than conflict and tension. Nicole later began sharing some of the ways in which her trauma had affected her spirituality.

NICOLE: *I was raised a Baptist and went to church regularly with my parents, but after the abuse I would sit in the pews and think that God didn't care about me. God let all kinds of bad things happen to people. I still feel that life isn't fair. How is there any justice or goodness in the world if innocent girls can be violated? I don't know how to get back my faith.*

Only you know how your traumatic experience has shaped the way you see yourself, your sense of purpose and meaning in life. Trauma challenges your fundamental beliefs, and you may still be struggling with what the traumatic experience has meant for you. You may also have found some answers, and feel that you have grown in important ways from the experience. Sharing all of this is a powerful way to reconnect with those you love.

Share How You've Been Working To Overcome PTSD

Not only should you talk about how the trauma has affected you, you should also share how you have been working to overcome your PTSD. You have tremendous courage and strength to endure PTSD. You have many natural coping strategies that have helped you, and you are working hard to learn more. Talk about your efforts, your successes, and your setbacks.

DAN: *Drinking was the quick fix for me. In the beginning, it felt like the only way to calm myself down, and I thought it would help me fall asleep. But I found that I still had nightmares about the war, and I would smoke pot in the day whenever the memory of the explosion would start running through my mind like a videotape. I could tell the drinking and weed were like Band-Aids or worse. When I started really working on things in therapy, I discovered that I could handle the mem-*

ories, I could face my fears. I stopped using drugs and drinking beer altogether. I worked on my avoidance so that I was better at going to crowded games, restaurants, movie theaters. I'm not totally there yet, but I'm a heck of a lot better than I was six months ago!

NICOLE: All I know is that I became one tough cookie. I survived growing up by taking no one's crap, working really hard at school, keeping my distance. I had some friends, but I learned how to be on my own. This was my strength. It got me through, and taught me that I could always take care of myself. Now I'm trying to find that softer part of myself that I have kept safe inside. I am learning how to let more of my feelings show, and to try to open up more with Peter. I'm working hard on it in therapy, but I also think we can work together on this. Instead of fighting, it feels like we can form a united front.

Explain What You Want from Them

Before you talk about your trauma experience, think about what you want from the other person. Most people simply want the other person to listen and understand their experience. The important thing to remember, however, is that they may not be able to completely get what it was like for you if they haven't gone through the same thing. What you should ask for is that they *try* to understand. It is their effort to empathize that matters.

You should also make it clear whether or not you want any feedback or advice from them. Most people with PTSD don't want advice. They already know more about their condition than anyone else, they understand what they need to focus on, and they know how hard they are working at it. The reason listeners will be pulled to give you advice or try to solve the problem for you is that it is hard for them to see you suffer, and they genuinely want to help.

But usually, advice doesn't help: It can feel impatient and controlling. And there are no quick fixes with PTSD. Gently explain to the listener that advice or solutions are not what you are seeking—you just want him or her to listen and try to understand.

Sometimes, you may want their help with a specific aspect of your recovery, which is fine to make clear. You may want their assistance in doing some exposure exercises (see chapter 4), or helping you reduce your drinking or practice relaxation techniques. You may ask them to learn more about PTSD, read some of the chapters in this book, or attend a therapy session with you. You need to state what specific thing you want from them in a given conversation.

Putting It All Together

Sometimes it is helpful to think through your conversation about PTSD beforehand, especially if it is the first time you have talked about it with your family member or friend. The following is a summary of what we've included in the chapter, to help you structure the conversation. You don't have to include all of this in one conversation, but always start by giving the listener a heads-up and telling him or her what you would like to talk about and what you want from them. At the end of this chapter, we have also provided tips for friends and family who want to know how they can be even better listeners.

Steps to Structuring the Conversation

1. **Give them a heads-up and check in:**

   - *I'd like to talk to you about how I've been coping with a traumatic experience I had.*

- *I won't be talking about the details of the trauma.*

- *Instead, I want to tell you about how it has affected me and what I've been doing to overcome PTSD.*

- *Are you okay with that? Is this a good time to talk?*

2. **Explain what you want from them:**

- *I want you to listen and try to understand.*

- *I don't want advice or suggestions on how to solve the problem.*

- *I would like you to [read the chapter about PTSD, practice a skill with me].*

3. **Name the trauma, but don't go into details:**

- *I was abused by my uncle.*

- *I was in combat in Iraq. I lost a close buddy.*

- *Last year I was mugged after work.*

- *I was in New Orleans when Katrina hit.*

- *I was in a serious car accident.*

- *I was almost killed fighting a fire, and was unable to save someone.*

4. **Talk about your struggle with PTSD:**

- *Afterwards, I was anxious all the time. I had trouble sleeping. I had trouble concentrating at work.*

- *I swung between fear and anger. I was always snapping at my kids.*

- *I really struggled with nightmares and memories of the event. I started drinking so I could calm down and get to sleep.*

- *I withdrew from my family and friends. It was so hard to be around other people.*

- *I couldn't go to ball games or movies anymore.*

- *I had trouble dating. Any kind of physical touch felt awful.*

- *My grades dropped. I couldn't work, so I left my job.*

5. **Share how the trauma has affected your beliefs and sense of self:**

- *At first I felt like something was wrong with me, that I was bad. Later, I developed a tough exterior, excelled at school, and kept to myself.*

- *I didn't think life was fair. I started doubting the existence of God.*

- *I had always felt pretty competent, especially as a soldier. But after Iraq, I didn't feel so powerful anymore.*

- *Am I a good or moral person if I failed to save my buddy?*

- *Why was Cesar killed, while I survived? It doesn't feel right that I got to come home to my wife and my kids, and he didn't.*

6. **Describe how you've been working to overcome PTSD:**

- *I've been working on how to manage anxiety using my mind and relaxation, instead of alcohol. I'm six-months sober.*

- *I'm practicing exposure exercises to get rid of my fear of crowds, so that I can start going to ball games and concerts.*

- *My "tough-cookie" attitude helped me survive when I was young. Now I'm trying to develop my softer side, and for the first time in my life, know what real intimacy is.*

- *I'm learning to accept what happened to me. In a way, this work has really made me stronger.*

- *I'm working on my sleep habits, so I'm not so exhausted in the day.*

- *I've been writing about how I have also grown from this experience.*

7. **Tell them how much you appreciate being able to talk to them:**

   - *I really appreciate being able to talk to you about this.*

   - *Thank you for listening, and trying to understand.*

   - *I feel better having shared this with you.*

Some Tips for the Listener

This section is for you, the family member or friend of someone who has PTSD and wants to talk about his or her experience. There are several things you can do to really help out and be supportive.

The first is to focus on trying to understand the person's experience and feelings. Even though you have not gone through the traumatic experience yourself or had to struggle with PTSD, your desire to understand can really go a long way.

To be supportive and helpful, it is not essential that you know the details of what happened. Your intention matters. Your caring matters. Your effort to listen matters. You can do all that without ever knowing the precise sequence of events. You don't have to know exactly what occurred in order to empathize with the trauma survivor's experience. It is useful to just try to grasp the feelings, the meaning, and the effect on him or her.

One way to do this is to repeat or paraphrase what the person says. This helps to make sure that you understand his meaning, and to let him know how closely you are listening. It also helps to focus on the person's feelings rather than the facts, so try to talk to him about his grief, sadness, fear, anger, and hopelessness. This can be hard, but it is a powerful way to be there for the person.

You may feel pulled to give advice or try to solve the person's problems. Resist this temptation. People often want to jump in and give advice because it is hard to feel the pain of the trauma survivor. You want to take away those bad feelings so that he or she feels better—and you feel better, too. While you may be trying to be helpful with your advice, it generally doesn't feel that way to the other person. Rest assured that they are working hard on their PTSD and have a lot of knowledge and skill already. Getting over PTSD is much like recovering from a serious physical disease. Let the person work with his or her therapist or doctor to take care of the symptoms: You provide the caring. When they feel understood and accepted, you will be helping them not only get closer to you, but also providing the healing effects of social support. You can ask them if there are additional ways that you can be helpful, but if listening is all they need from you, rest assured that this is a profound way you can help.

It's also important to keep in mind all of your loved one's

strengths as you listen to his or her struggle. Any one of us can develop PTSD after a trauma, and it takes enormous energy and courage to overcome it. Always treat the person with dignity and respect—he or she is not weak, sick, or helpless. While it is natural to feel impatient with people who may not be getting better as quickly as you want, be careful not to judge or be critical. The trauma survivor is on a hard road, and really needs your support. Listen to him or her with an open, nonjudgmental, and empathetic attitude. Encourage the survivor to talk about how he or she has been working to overcome PTSD. Remember always to keep in mind the whole person.

Summary of the listening tips:

1. **Listen and try to understand.**

   - Let him or her do most of the talking.

   - Try to be warm, open, and accepting.

   - Repeat or paraphrase what the person is saying.

   - Focus on what he or she is feeling.

2. **Don't give advice or try to fix the problem.**

   - Try not to give advice unless specifically asked for it.

   - Don't try to fix the problem or change the person.

   - Don't try to make their bad feelings go away.

   - Don't be critical, judgmental, or focus on his or her faults.

   - Don't try to be their doctor.

Moving Forward

Sharing how your trauma has affected your life is a profoundly connecting experience. We have provided you a structured way to do this, by talking about what you've been struggling with and what you've learned through your recovery. Notice that the trauma conversation includes both negative and positive aspects of your experience. While previous chapters can help you put words to your PTSD symptoms and how trauma has challenged your core beliefs, the final chapter of this book can help you better understand how you've developed through the experience. PTSD is not just struggle; it is also a path to discovering your strengths and perhaps even new goals. We invite you in the next chapter to explore how trauma can lead to meaningful growth in your life.

CHAPTER 13

Using Trauma as an Opportunity to Grow

Ian

The moment the muggers caught him, Ian believed he was going to die. In an instant, he thought about his parents, how he'd never traveled to Europe or been married, all the things he still wanted to do in his life. He wasn't ready to go. For a few days afterward, he felt so lucky to be alive. Every moment was a gift. Then the anxiety started to take over his life, and it became very hard for him to deal with the symptoms. But as he developed skills for managing the anxiety, he started thinking about that moment of insight—that life is precious. Ian decided to develop strategies to hold on to that gratitude in his life, and not take anything for granted. He found it gave him a richer sense of being alive.

■

Angela

Angela had lost her way after Hurricane Katrina. She struggled with the death of her mother and PTSD, and for years felt afraid and uncertain. But as she learned to manage her anxiety and work through her grief, she realized that she needed to rebuild a sense of connection and meaning in her new home. Drawing on her personal experience, Angela began to volunteer to help survivors of local disasters. She recognized the confusion in people's eyes after a household fire, and she found that she could rally their strength and determination to get through it. Over time, she rediscovered her enthusiasm for living and her ability to inspire others. Her trauma and her mother's death had helped her define a new purpose: helping others in need.

■

For Ian, the terror of that moment left a deep imprint in his soul—without warning, he faced his mortality. It left him with PTSD, but it also left him with a new sense of how precious life is. For Angela, having experienced the destruction and loss of Katrina made her re-evaluate what mattered to her. She realized she wanted to spend her time and talents in the service of others who had gone through similar traumas.

When trauma pulls the rug out from under you, there is always a period of disorientation and struggle. Beliefs are challenged, symptoms of anxiety and depression emerge, former activities are temporarily or permanently given up. You may even lose friends and loved ones. But as you recover, a silver lining often emerges from the black cloud. You might discover a new sense of your strengths, the value of your relationships, or a deeper appreciation of what you treasure in life. You may learn to lean on others and discover new ways to give to your loved ones, friends, and community. In trauma's wake, you are often able to grow in profound ways as a human being.

How To Grow from Your Trauma

Growing from trauma starts with the recognition that there are things in your life you cannot control, and aspects of your life that you do have the power to change. You don't have control over the fact that you experienced a life-threatening or horrifying experience, and that it deeply affected your life. But you do have control over how you view your trauma, what it eventually comes to mean in your life, and whether you grow from the experience.

Growing from trauma has two components: acceptance and action. Acceptance is required because you have experienced a traumatic event and possibly a loss. If, before the trauma, you felt invulnerable in life, there will be a new recognition that you are indeed vulnerable, and there are forces outside of your control—acts of nature, accidents, the actions of others—that can deeply affect your life.

But *you* are in charge of the meaning of these events in your life, and how you live your life in response to them. Do you view the trauma as a defeat or a challenge? Are you able to move from victim to one who can make a difference in people's lives? The meaning you bring to your life does not exist somewhere outside of yourself: You create it from within. You have the power to place your trauma into your life narrative, and make it a turning point in how you feel about yourself and how you interact with others and the world.

Many people have found that their traumas helped them grow into wiser, stronger, and more compassionate human beings. This growth enabled them to give back to others—to contribute to their families and communities in new ways, and make a difference in others' lives. Learning how to grow from your traumatic experience requires that you distinguish between when to act and when to let go. It requires grieving your losses and accepting the things in your life that have changed for good, and having the courage, creativity, and will to develop yourself and give in ways you have control over. Remember that courage doesn't exist when you are safe and things are fine in your life. Courage is expressed only when you are afraid, but put yourself out there anyway.

The rest of this chapter is dedicated to helping you tap into and develop your resiliency, growth, and connection to others.

Using Trauma as a Wake-Up Call to Living Life More Fully

For Ian, his near-death experience brought into sharp focus how valuable his life was to him. He recognized how easy it was to take everything—his great job, his physical health, his cool apartment in New York, his loving and supportive parents, even his German shepherd—for granted. Realizing how he might have lost these parts of his life during the mugging left him profoundly grateful for his life.

In his book *Existential Psychotherapy*, Dr. Irving Yalom wrote extensively about how facing death can enable you to live a fuller and more authentic life. He believed that everyone has a fear of his own mortality, but normally people defend against this awareness because of the anxiety it produces. We avoid this reality by simply not thinking about our own death or the death of those we love. Instead, most of us carry a protective belief that nothing bad will happen to us. Trauma strips that assumption away, revealing a truth that is very painful to accept: Everyone, including ourselves, will die. This is the existential reality we all face. Only when one is diagnosed with a potentially fatal illness or almost loses his or her life in a trauma does one deal with this reality directly.

Yalom, working with people diagnosed with cancer and other life-threatening illnesses, saw that this death awareness in his patients was also a vehicle for becoming more alive and connected in the world. In other words, facing the reality that we are truly vulnerable—that all of us will lose loved ones and will eventually die ourselves—can be the impetus to growth. Many people who have looked death in the eye have used this awareness to appreciate what is dear to them. The impact has been to reinvigorate their lives, deepen their gratitude, and heighten their ability to savor the beauty and wonder in life.

Journal Exercise: How Has Trauma Opened Your Eyes?

How has trauma been a wake-up call for you? Are there people or aspects of life that you have a new appreciation for? And how do you hold on to that sense of how precious life is?

Daily Gratitude Exercise: Savoring the Moment

Even after a life-threatening trauma, at some point people find themselves slipping back into their everyday lives, forgetting to notice and appreciate what is most valuable to them. There is a simple exercise that you can do each day to make sure you stop to smell the roses, notice a sunset or a smile, and enhance your sense of aliveness and appreciation. You can use your journal to do the exercise, or start a separate daily gratitude book.

In the evening, say, think, or write down:

- Something in your day that moved you or inspired you.

- Something you did for yourself or others today that you can acknowledge.

- Someone you are grateful for in your life, and what you appreciate about him or her.

Using Trauma to Increase Connection with Others

Part of trauma's wake-up call involves recognizing how important your partner, family members, and friends are in your life. Many people who have experienced a life-threatening trauma report a greater appreciation for their loved ones, making every moment together precious. And as you share more about your experience with others—how you have changed, your struggles with PTSD, what it means in your life—you deepen your intimacy even more.

Trauma can inspire the communication of true emotion. You open up and talk about what's real and meaningful. This change is often more pronounced in men, who before the trauma may have kept their feelings to themselves. Many also find that they feel more connected to other people's suffering. You may have noticed that you are more empathetic as you listen to others, and strive in new ways to provide understanding and support. In all these ways, trauma enhances the value you place on relationships and how you relate to others.

This doesn't mean that people with PTSD don't also struggle with their relationships. As we discussed in section 3, it is common for trauma survivors to feel alienated from others at first, or to experience anger or mistrust. But as you work through these relationship difficulties and learn to reconnect, you will often recognize that underneath your struggle with others is a new and profound recognition of their importance to you. The key is to increase this awareness, and to express gratitude for the people in your life.

Here's how Barry was able to do this over time:

BARRY: As I said, after the fire I felt pretty removed from my wife and daughters. The anxiety and depression settled in, and I just didn't want to be around anyone. I was also really afraid that something would happen to them, and I tried to shove that down. I didn't need more to worry about. Then, one day, I was watching Shaundra dress our daughter, Melanie, before school, just like she always did. Only I noticed Shaundra's hands—how gentle and loving she was as she buttoned Melanie's dress. They were smiling at each other. And suddenly I just felt so much joy looking at them. And I thought, this is what I should be paying attention to every day. I remember choking up a bit, and then feeling really certain: This is why we are here on this planet. Now I look for those moments, so they don't pass me by. And I try to tell Shaundra what an amazing mom and wife she is.

Trauma survivors also learn that they can really depend on some of the people in their lives. They discover that loved ones come through for them or that even friends and people at work or school care about what happened to them.

Ian's coworkers would stop by his desk periodically to check with him the first month after the assault; some offered to take him to lunch or help out with his work. Later, as Ian developed PTSD, it was his boss who encouraged him to seek treatment. Angela's sister cleared out a room in her house so that Angela could move in and stay until she got back on her feet. Nicole realized that Peter would stand by her and provide consistent support as she struggled through her abuse history and learned to reconnect.

After your trauma, who did you call or go to see? Are there friends or family members who have provided help and support during your struggle with PTSD?

For some people, it's hard to ask for help. When Dan first got back from Iraq, he knew he was having a hard time, but he didn't talk about it with his wife. He was afraid she would see him as weak, and as the months went by and his anxiety and avoidance got worse, he became even more worried that he would become dependent on her. Later, as he learned more about PTSD in his veterans group and in individual therapy, he realized that the symptoms were not an indication of weakness, but a common response to an uncommon experience such as combat. This made it easier for him to risk opening up to Heather, and he used some of the techniques discussed in chapter 12 to start sharing his experience. To Dan's surprise, Heather responded with relief and heartfelt support. The conversation made her feel valuable and important in being able to give to him, and Dan found that they grew closer because of it.

Leaning on others is a sign of growth, because it shows that you are confident enough within yourself to let another help you; men especially aren't often encouraged to develop this trait while growing up. But it's important to know that when you ask for help, you not only share more of your authentic self, you also provide an opportunity for the other person to feel useful, trusted, and significant in your life. Until you take the risk of opening up to loved ones and requesting their help with overcoming your anxiety, depression, or avoidance, you haven't really let them into your inner world. You are struggling, as they are; learning to be a mutual support system for one another will strengthen you and your relationships.

Practice: Increasing Connection with Others

- Recognize the people in your life who are your support system, and acknowledge them.

- Take time to appreciate moments of connection.

- Open up with others, share what is genuine and real about yourself.

- Work through your relationship conflicts in order to increase mutual understanding and support.

- Be willing to lean on others; give them the opportunity to help you.

Using Acceptance and Honoring to Grow from Loss

Trauma often involves loss. You may have experienced the death of a family member or friend, or a change in some physical ability if you were injured, or even feel that you have lost some aspect of yourself. To grow from these tangible and symbolic losses, you must be able to grieve, which is one of the hardest things to do in post-traumatic growth work. Grieving involves accepting that your loss is real, and letting yourself feel sadness and related emotions that naturally arise. It involves letting go of what you cannot change—the person or the quality that was part of you that you cannot get back. Especially, grieving involves honoring who you lost.

Angela's mother was killed during Katrina, and Dan lost Cesar, his friend and fellow soldier in Iraq. [Sometimes the loss is not a death or injury, but more symbolic.] Those who survived a war or disaster with a head injury or debilitating wounds may find that the kind of work they can do or how they relate to others has changed forever. If, like Nicole, you experienced a trauma in childhood, you may have lost your innocence, sense of being protected, or part of your childhood by having grown up too quickly. Sonya lost the ability to use her left arm in the accident, and had to relearn how to do so many activities that others take for granted. Additional losses that sometimes can occur well after a trauma (such as having a parent, friend, or even a pet pass away) can also reactivate your PTSD. Whether the loss was part of your trauma or came afterwards, it is important to do the work of grieving. Usually, though, people need some time to recover from the trauma and get their symptoms under control before they have the emotional space to do grief work.

Unfortunately, some people never work through their grief, even after a lot of time has passed. You may fear that if you allow yourself to feel the pain of the loss, you will be overwhelmed with grief and never stop crying, or that you will fall apart. Giving in to your grief may also feel like weakness, especially if you are male.

At the time of the trauma, it can sometimes be adaptive to shut down your feelings in order to cope effectively. When Dan realized that Cesar had been killed in the explosion, he went completely numb. In the chaos and confusion, Dan was calm and focused as he fanned out with the rest of his platoon to search for insurgents. But avoiding the grief can become a problem afterwards. Following Cesar's death, Dan attempted to keep thoughts about him away by drinking heavily during the rest of his tour in Iraq and later, when he returned home.

The problem is, *not grieving* takes a tremendous amount of energy, and the pain doesn't really go away. It lurks in the back of your consciousness like a ghost, haunting you. Defending against the sadness and pain also makes it difficult to feel open and alive, to have positive feelings such as joy, love, happiness, excitement, humor. There is no way to turn off the negative feelings alone. There is really only one emotional faucet in your brain, which means you end up turning off *all* feelings when you try to shut out pain.

The good news is that there are ways to work through your loss, and you will not fall apart by doing the work. You will experience sadness, you will cry, but you will not cry forever. The willingness to face your grief is actually a strength rather than a weakness, and you will find that once you begin, you have the courage to do it. Most importantly, working through your loss will bring great relief and meaning to your life and those you mourn.

This brings us to a critical last point. Many people who have lost a friend or relative feel that if they work through their grief and move on, somehow they are not being fair or respectful to the person who has died. But truly grieving is how you honor the deceased. It doesn't mean you stop missing them, or forget about them. It means that you work to accept their deaths, to remember what they contributed to others and the world, and perhaps to use their lives as inspiration to help others and create more meaning in your own life.

We've included three grief exercises below. The first involves writing a letter to someone who has died as a way of saying goodbye and honoring his or her life. You can also write a letter to yourself, expressing your feelings about some part of you that was lost. The second exercise involves honoring the deceased with a ritual or remembrance. The final exercise focuses on using the life of the deceased as an inspiration to do something positive in your life.

Grieving Exercise 1: Writing a Letter to the Deceased (or a Lost Part of Yourself)

Letters are a powerful way to remember someone who has died. You can use the letter to express your sense of loss and pain. But it is just as important to use the letter as a way to honor the individual, to express what he or she contributed to your life and to others. Every human being—even those who lived only a short time—has made a difference in the world. How do you want to remember them? Were they particularly good at giving love and support, or standing by you with steadfast loyalty? Did they know how to challenge others and inspire them? Were they fair, unassuming, and kind? What difference did they make at home and at work? Did they give to their families, communities, or to their country? What has it been like for you without them? How have you missed them?

Here is Angela's letter to her mom:

Momma,

You've been gone three years now. There are so many things I want to say to you. I wish that I had spent more time with you over the last years of your life, because you were a wise and strong woman. And you were generous with your family—even while teaching and raising five screaming children that paid you no mind half the time. You knew how to be tough but you were loving, too. I remember so many little things: how you would cook my favorite spicy gumbo on my birthday, or the way you'd lift your eyebrow when you didn't believe me, giving me time to change my story. And how you knitted the softest blankets for everyone in the family. I lost that blanket and everything else in the floodwaters after Katrina, but I remember the red and yellow design like it was right in front of me. I wish I had told you how much I admired you. But I will remember you every day of my life. I will remember the one who brought me into this world, took care of me, and showed me how to be strong and kind. I will use your memory as my inspiration, as I fight my way back and start a new life.

Your loving daughter,
Angela

If your loss was not a person but a part of you, write a letter to yourself. Nicole did need to acknowledge and grieve her lost childhood. She wrote about how her withdrawal from others made it difficult to make friends in middle and high school, how she lost out on so many important moments related to being a teenager—her first dance, first kiss, being on a sports team, having a best friend. But, like Angela, she not only wrote about loss, she also wrote about her strengths, and how she was able to get through those years. Sonya, in her letter to herself, expressed her pain over losing the ability to use her left arm and all the activities she could no longer easily do. She also wrote about how she is working to overcome her disability, but the focus of this letter centered on accepting and grieving the loss.

Grieving Exercise 2: Creating a Ritual or Remembrance to Honor the Deceased

Instead of writing a letter to Cesar, Dan decided to put together a remembrance book for Cesar's parents. He was inspired by paintings of the men and women who were killed in Iraq—the "Faces of the Fallen" exhibit at Arlington National Cemetery. Dan contacted other soldiers in his unit and asked them for stories, photos, and descriptions of Cesar. Even those who were still deployed in Iraq emailed anecdotes to Dan.

A memory book can be one way to honor the deceased, but even smaller rituals can be a meaningful way to remember him or her, such as setting aside a spot in your home to display a photo and personal objects of the individual. Rituals can also help you get through anniversaries of the person's death; you can take out pictures of the person and share a few stories, or go to a special spot on that day and think about him or her. Along with writing a letter, other ways to say goodbye might be leaving a stone at a quiet spot in the woods, or casting a token remembrance into a pond or the ocean.

Grieving Exercise 3: Using the Life of the Deceased as Inspiration for Action

Those who have died are not gone from our hearts. We keep them alive in our memories, where they can inspire us to change things for the better. When Dan looked through the stories and pictures of Cesar, he thought about how Cesar used to boost morale by telling jokes and getting people to talk or play cards during stressful times. Would Cesar have wanted Dan to stay stuck in the past, or live his own life and help others? Dan realized that he could honor Cesar's life by reaching out to his fellow veterans. Cesar inspired him to begin talking about PTSD, and to bring together other veterans to provide support to one another.

You can honor the memory of a friend or loved one by using his or her life as an inspiration for new action, such as:

- Taking up a cause.

- Taking on a new challenge.

- Volunteering to help others.

- Committing to making some positive change in yourself.

Recognizing Your Strengths and Virtues

While trauma shines a spotlight on your vulnerability, it also reveals strengths you didn't realize you possessed. There are many moving stories from the September 11th terrorist attack of New Yorkers rushing to help others, comforting one another on the streets, and pulling together as a community. There are similar stories of courage and compassion during every major disaster around the world.

Angela, although distraught about her mother, still created games to distract frightened kids in the Superdome, as they waited out the hurricane; she also befriended an elderly survivor who was frightened and alone. Disasters wreak havoc and are terrifying, but like any trauma, large or small, they also require people to tap into their individual strengths to pull through and help others. Even when people feel they are falling apart, somehow they still do what they need to do in order to survive.

The *Merriam-Webster's Collegiate® Dictionary* defines courage as "mental or moral strength to venture, persevere, and withstand danger, fear, or difficulty." Notice that you can't display courage when you are safe or in your comfort zone; it is only expressed in moments of fear and danger. No matter how you responded during the trauma itself, you withstood and persevered in the face of that threat.

Many people also discover their courage *after* the trauma, during the time of recovery and coping. People with PTSD learn that they can withstand intense anxiety in order to work, go to school, or take care of family. And if you have actively worked on overcoming avoidance of situations that trigger anxiety (described in chapter 4) or the trauma memory itself (chapter 11), then you have truly learned that you can survive facing your fears. You also develop a thicker skin and discover that you are tougher than you thought. If you are recovering from a trauma, you should recognize and acknowledge the courage you have already demonstrated, as you continue to fight to get your life back and do the difficult work of recovering from PTSD.

Sonya struggled for a long time after the trauma, not only with intense anxiety and avoidance, but also with learning how to cope without the use of her left arm. She had to muster the strength to face her fears and to overcome her new disability. She discovered along the way that she indeed had that courage, and also a level of perseverance, dependability, and competence that surprised her.

> SONYA: I never thought that I'd have to figure out how to live with a disability. But I discovered that I had a kind of strength I never knew I had. I learned how to type with one hand, make coffee, eat, cook, and play with Eric. You don't realize how you depend on two hands to do most things! Learning took incredible effort and creativity, and there was more than once I wanted to throw myself on the couch and give up. But I believe I was given this challenge to learn from it. And I did it, even while fighting the PTSD. My next goal is to start driving regularly to work. I've already overcome my fear of being in a car again, and I'll learn to drive one-handed! My friend calls me "wonder woman" and you know, I'm going to prove her right!

People discover many sources of resiliency in themselves during their recoveries from trauma. It is common for people to get in touch with a more genuine emotional side of themselves, and to open up and connect more deeply with others. Some develop a new commitment to contribute to others, volunteer for a cause, or fight for justice. Nicole had spent all the years since her childhood abuse distancing herself from others, in an effort to protect herself. Until her relationship with Peter, she didn't feel safe letting others in. She had developed a tough exterior and maintained her distance. But as she started opening up to Peter, she began to develop a new sense of herself as a kind and lovable woman—one who is capable of having emotionally close relationships.

NICOLE: I had to feel differently inside myself before I could reach out. Before, it was all about keeping people out. But now that I feel safer, more solid, I want to be open and let them in. I want to share what's going on. And I am better at listening to Peter when he's had a hard day, or to my friends when they are stressed or heartbroken. I am so incredibly grateful for this. I feel connected to humanity for the first time in my life. And lately I've been thinking about how I can help others who have been abused. I know now that relationships are how you heal from this.

Many people report after trauma that they feel wiser and more experienced. They have confronted death, a loss, or a severe challenge, and they have learned from it. In Buddhist philosophy, suffering is a universal experience, and you can use it to connect in a deeper, more authentic way with your loved ones and humanity. Trauma can be a source of wisdom and compassion, and a bridge to others.

Martin Seligman has written about the idea that everyone has his or her own "signature strengths." However you define your own unique strengths, they become your core source of resiliency during stressful or traumatic times. They are also the seeds of your posttraumatic growth. Here is a summary of some of the strengths people often discover about themselves after going through a traumatic experience:

- Courage

- Perseverance

- Dependability

- Competence

- Connection to humanity

- Justice

- Love

- Loyalty and commitment

- Optimism

- Humor

- Forgiveness

- Selflessness

- Wisdom and experience

- Spirituality

Journal Exercise: Your Discovered Strengths

Write about those positive aspects of yourself that you have discovered—or are further developing—following your traumatic experience. What strengths has your trauma revealed in you?

Growing by Contributing to Others

Not only do trauma survivors learn that they can depend on other people in their life, they often find at some point in their recovery that they want to help others. This desire may arise through the experience of shared suffering, a new appreciation for how precious life and relationships are, or the discovery of one's strengths during the process of recovery.

There are many ways to contribute to your family or community. Dan, inspired by Cesar's memory, took it upon himself to talk to veterans' groups about PTSD, and also helped publicize veteran support groups. He wanted to communicate what he had learned about the effects of combat trauma, and he wanted to help other vets who might be struggling alone. Angela also felt that she could use her experience in Katrina to help other disaster survivors, so she became an American Red Cross volunteer who responded to local disaster emergencies in her city. Sonya used her newfound sense of competency and perseverance to volunteer at her son's school and also to raise money for the school's art program. Other trauma survivors emerge from their experiences with a passion to fight for certain causes that affect people's lives, such as reducing violence in their communities, advocating for cancer research funding, or fighting for human rights and social justice.

However your desire to contribute to others emerges following a trauma, it can be deeply healing and meaningful. The act of helping can be empowering, especially if you have struggled with fear, loss of control, or feelings of helplessness because of your PTSD. Helping also increases your personal sense of value and usefulness: Even if you are anxious or depressed, you still have something to give. Small acts of gratitude and appreciation are also ways you can contribute to others. When you find ways of sharing your wisdom and skills to help others, you remind yourself of your strengths—and that you have grown from your trauma experience. This creates a new sense of purpose and meaning in your life.

Here are some of the ways you can contribute to your family, friends, community, or broader human causes. Some of these we talked about in chapter 8. You can give in small or large ways—any act of extending yourself is a positive step toward growth.

Family and Friends

- Surprise your partner by making a special dinner.

- Leave your partner a note with some acknowledgement or expression of gratitude.

- Volunteer to babysit for a friend or to help a family member with some task.

- Volunteer to help fix or repair something.

- Ask about someone's day, and really listen.

- Offer emotional or tangible support for someone having a hard day.

Community

- Volunteer at your local school, art or music program, nature center.

- Start a support group.

- Volunteer at a homeless shelter or food bank.

- Give blood, contribute to a local fundraising effort, donate books to your library.

- Teach students to read.

- Donate your carpentry, legal, financial, artistic, or mental health skills to a nonprofit organization.

- Sponsor someone in a 12-step recovery program.

- Help people to start small businesses.

Humanitarian and Global

- Volunteer to help with environmental efforts.

- Join or start programs to reduce violence or poverty, or feed the hungry.

- Help raise money for programs to fight heart disease, cancer, asthma, or any illness that has touched you personally.

- Get involved in electing leaders you believe in.

- Fight for human rights and social or economic justice.

Journal Exercise: Contributing to Others

What are some of the ways you might want to contribute to your family, friends, community, or other causes?

Revising Your Philosophy of Life and Creating New Goals

Trauma puts things in perspective. If you were told that you only had a few years to live, what would you choose to do? Or if you were on your deathbed, looking back over your life, what would seem most important?

All the ways that people grow through trauma naturally translate into a revised philosophy of life, as people often change their priorities and goals with the recognition that life is short and relationships precious. Commonly, this involves a shift away from an emphasis on work or societal markers of achievement—making more money, acquiring material goods, achieving greater social status—and toward a greater focus on relationships and contributing to others. The life-changing experience of trauma may also be the catalyst to go back to school or change careers.

The effort to recreate your beliefs about the world and your purpose in life can be complicated by spiritual turmoil. In chapter 10, we explored how people's faith can be shaken by trauma. For those who are spiritual or religious, there is often a period of questioning how one's Higher Power could have allowed for such suffering. It is a long and difficult process to find understanding following a traumatic experience. But some find meaning in the ways they have grown through adversity. They feel that the trauma was a spiritual wake-up call for them, one that changed their paths in life and their priorities. They see their deeply personal journey of recovery from trauma as changing them for the better.

Barry recognized that he was detached from his family even before the tragic fire. As he struggled with his depression and PTSD, he discovered that he was not invulnerable—that no one was, and that he was missing what mattered in life. He might have lived out his days without ever really *seeing* his wife and daughter, and he believed God meant to give him this new vision. Angela found spiritual meaning in her Katrina experience as well. She believes her traumatic experience revealed her true purpose in life: to help and comfort others in life-threatening disasters and emergencies. Nicole continues to struggle with her faith, but she has started to wonder whether God meant her to learn how to overcome her fear and anger in order to trust and love another human being. So while trauma can challenge your spirituality, it can often lead to a renewed and even strengthened sense of faith.

This chapter has focused on acceptance of loss and change, recognition of your strengths and virtues, and the creation of positive meaning in your life through revised priorities and contributing to others. You cannot erase the fact that you experienced a trauma, but you can imbue your heart with a sense of purpose and commitment. As you contemplate what you value most about yourself and your life, think about how you can put these values into action. Here are some of the revised goals of our six individuals whose experiences with PTSD were described throughout this book:

New Goals Based on Revised Priorities and Philosophy of Life

IAN	1. Spend more time with my parents, and deepen my relationship with them.
	2. Get to know my colleagues at work as people, and reconnect with friends I've lost touch with.
	3. Don't take life for granted: Live each day to the fullest, and use gratitude exercises to remember life is short and precious.
ANGELA	1. Find ways to remember and honor my mother.
	2. Volunteer to help local and national disaster survivors.
	3. Get my B.A. so that I can change careers and work with emergency response teams.
DAN	1. Reach out to other veterans about PTSD.
	2. Start making films about war, military sacrifice, and the consequences.
	3. Improve my relationship with my family by continuing to work on my anger and improving how I communicate my needs and feelings.
	4. Stay sober.

SONYA	1. Volunteer at my daughter's school.
	2. Learn how to drive (overcome anxiety and disability!).
	3. Develop a career raising money for important causes.
BARRY	1. Continue to open up more with my wife, and bring more romance into our marriage.
	2. Appreciate and express gratitude to my family.
	3. Develop new friendships with men who I can be genuine with.
NICOLE	1. Keep working every day to build trust and connection with my fiancé and close friends.
	2. Start going to church again.

As your last entry in your journal, take time to think about what new goals you want to create for yourself.

Journal Exercise: Your Gouls

Think about your strengths and sources of resiliency, and what you have learned through your trauma experience. Then use this knowledge to commit to goals you really believe in. Write these in your journal.

Moving Forward—Your Ongoing Journey

This book has taken you on a journey from trauma toward growth. It began with learning about the struggles that emerge following trauma—the symptoms of anxiety, avoidance, and depression, the harmful ways people sometimes cope with drugs and alcohol, the relationship difficulties. You have learned about the nature of these problems, and developed strategies for overcoming them. Next, you moved on to confronting the trauma itself—the memories, the meaning of the event and how it's challenged your beliefs, and what you have discovered about yourself and your life. Finally, you've learned how to draw on your trauma experience to transform your life in positive ways.

The work of recovery and growth is ongoing. At a minimum, it involves fighting to conquer the symptoms of PTSD every day. But you can also use trauma to recognize your strengths and values, connect more deeply with others, and commit to new life goals. It is difficult but deeply fulfilling work. We salute you for rebuilding your life with courage, inspiration, and action—and we wish you well on the rest of your journey.

Acknowledgments

I would first like to thank the individuals with PTSD whom I have had the honor to work with; they have taught me much about courage and resilience. I am also grateful to my mentors and colleagues in the trauma field (past and present) for their wisdom, consultation, and support for this book: Charles Marmar, David Mohr, Suzanne Best, Michael Telch, Ginger Rhodes, Sabra Inslicht & Shannon McCaslin. A special thanks to Loren Krane and Frank Schoenfeld for their editorial suggestions, and to Chuck Bussey for being an inspiration for my trauma work. In addition, this book would not have happened without my coauthor John Arden, whose passion and unflagging positive attitude helped to create a delightful collaboration.

I am especially indebted to those closest to me, whose love and encouragement saw me through this book. This includes my step-kids Casey and Kyle Lemle, who quickly made the leap from speechless shock ("you're writing what?") to unconditional and delighted support; the DC and NY Lemle clans lead by matron saint Peggy Lemle; and my amazing mom Jean Beckner, sister Holly Beckner, dear friend Erin Rogers, and nieces Lauren and Devon Magana, all for being my enduring cheerleaders.

Finally, deep gratitude goes to my husband, Russell Lemle. Thank you for the long and insightful conversations about our clinical work, your extensive editorial feedback on this book, and for eagerly doing all of the household chores while I was writing. Everything I do is made richer and more meaningful by your unwavering love.

—*Victoria Lemle Beckner, Ph.D.*

I would like to thank our skilled agent, Ed Knappman, for finding a great home for this book. His wise guidance over the years is greatly appreciated. Also, thanks go to Jill Alexander who was gracious and a pleasure to work with on this project. Finally, I would like to thank my coauthor whose expertise and intellectual vigor will undoubtedly bring her great success in the future.

—*John B. Arden, Ph.D.*

About the Authors

Victoria Lemle Beckner, Ph.D., is assistant clinical professor in the department of psychiatry at the University of California at San Francisco (UCSF) and a licensed psychologist with eleven years of experience in the areas of stress, anxiety disorders, and PTSD. She has provided PTSD treatment to military veterans at the San Francisco VA Medical Center and civilians through UCSF and her private practice. Her research involves testing new PTSD treatments for acute trauma and combat PTSD, and has published scholarly articles on how the stress hormone system affects memory and physical health. She teaches classes and workshops on the mind-body connection in psychiatric and medical conditions, cognitive behavioral therapy, and vicarious trauma. She was also invited to co-teach a course at the University of Rwanda on treatment approaches to trauma in the context of genocide. She volunteers her time in the community by providing pro-bono trauma services to victims of local and national disasters through the American Red Cross, is co-chair of the Disaster Response Network for the San Francisco Psychological Association, and represents psychologists on the statewide California Disaster Mental Health Coalition. She lives in Mill Valley, California.

John B. Arden, Ph.D., is the director of training for mental health for the Kaiser Permanente Medical Centers in northern California. In this capacity, he oversees one of the largest mental health training programs in the world. He has also previously served on the board of directors of a full-service domestic violence program and has worked with many women who have experienced PTSD as a result of domestic violence. He is the author or coauthor of nine other books, including *Brain-Based Therapy–Adult, Brain-Based Therapy–Child,* and *Heal Your Anxiety Workbook.* He lives in Sebastopol, California.

INDEX

anti-cholinergic side effects, 133

antidepressants, 115, 132–134, 137

antipsychotic medications, 132, 136, 137

anxiety, 10, 25, 27, 33, 38, 40, 67–68,
81–82, 84. *See also* panic attacks

anger and, 181

anxiety attacks, 97

anxiety disorders, 48

anxiety managemant, 159

anxiety scale, 46, 47, 76–77, 237

    coping strategies, 52–54

    development of, 71–74

    harmlessness of alarm sensations,
      50–52

    journaling and, 241

    medication for, 132

    reducing by modifying stress
      responses, 44–65

    relaxation techniques and, 57–65,
      150

    riding out, 46, 52–54, 237

    symptoms of, 46, 47

    tolerating, 150

    triggers of, 68–69, 69, 70–71, 74–75

anxiety attacks, 97

anxiety disorders, 48

anxiety management, 159

anxiety scale, 46, 47, 76–77, 237

appetite, change in, 86, 115, 124–125

assault, 20–21, 200–201. *See also* crime
victims

Ativan (lorazepam), 134, 135, 138

attention, 36, 87

atypical antipsychotic medications,
136, 137

avoidance, 37–38, 40

avoidance list, 76–78

    development of, 71–74

    overcoming by stepping out, 66–82

    triggers of, 68–71

avoidance list, 76–78

B

Barry, 18–19, 36–37, 83, 85, 97–100, 154,
156–157, 209–210, 218–219, 228, 271,
286, 288

behavioral activation techniques, 85

beliefs

    about control, 209–212

    about faith, 222–226

    about life purpose, 222–226

    about oneself, 212–218

    about power, 209–212

    about relationships, 218–222

    about safety, 205–208

    about the world, 222–226

    core beliefs, 201–203, 231

    effects of trauma on, 253–256, 258

    extreme beliefs, 203–204, 206–218

    narrative and, 240–241

    recreating, 285–288

    revising, 204–205

    self-beliefs, 212–218

    trauma and, 200–226

benzodiazepine, 132, 134–136, 138.
See also specific medications

bipolar disorder, 136

black or white thinking, 92–93

blaming, 186

boredom, 87

brain chemistry, exercise and, 108

identity, effects of trauma on, 253–256, 258

imagery
  intrusive, 21, 33, 34–35, 137, 231
  relaxation techniques and, 46, 62–63

imipramine. *See* Tofranil (imipramine)

immune system, 32

Inderal (propranolol), 137

insomnia, 36, 114, 116–124. *See* also sleep problems

intentional trauma, 22

interpretation of events, 91–92, 159–161
  anger and, 178–179

intrusive imagery, 21, 33, 34–35, 137, 231

intrusive memories, 21, 33, 37, 136

intrusive thoughts, 21, 137, 231

invitations, saying "yes" to, 162–163

irritability, 33, 36, 86, 114

isolation, 157. See also withdrawal

J

jitteriness, 31

journal exercises, 24. *See* also journaling
  avoidance list, 71
  contributing to others, 285
  goals, creating new, 288
  strengths, 282
  on substance use, 145, 146, 147
  talking about trauma, 248
  thought tables, 95, 99
  thought tables with realistic thoughts, 101–102
  trauma as a wake-up call, 269

journaling, 24, 228, 236–242. *See* also journal exercises
  anxiety and, 241
  time and setting of, 237–238

jumpiness, 36

L

Lamictal (lamotrigine), 136

lamotrigine. See Lamictal (lamotrigine)

L-Glutamine, 126

life purpose, 205
  beliefs about, 222–226
  effects of trauma on, 253–256, 258

light, 89, 109–111, 123

light-headedness, 30, 46

light-therapy devices, 111

lines, standing in, 70

listening, 194–195
  active, 168–169
  tips for, 261–264

lithium, 136

living more fully, 268–273

lorazepam. *See* Ativan (lorazepam)

L-Phenylalanine, 126

L-Tryptophan, 126

M

manic depression, 136

MAO inhibitors, 133, 134

medication, 115, 131–138. *See* also drugs; *specific medications*; substance use
  anti-cholinergic side effects, 133
  habit-forming, 134–136, 138, 139–151
  reducing dependence on, 139–151